1

Statistics Simplified

Learn to Make Better Decisions.
Become an Informed Consumer. Debunk
Popular Misbeliefs.

By Albert Rutherford and Abby Gordon
www.albertrutherford.com
albertrutherford@gmail.com

understanding that the author is not engaged in rendering medical, legal or other professional advice or services. If professional assistance is required, the services of a competent professional person should be sought. The author shall not be liable for damages arising herefrom. The fact that an individual, organization of website is referred to in this work as a citation and/or potential source of further information does not mean that the author endorses the information the individual, organization to the website may provide or recommendations they/it may make. Further, readers should be aware that Internet websites listed in this work might have changed or disappeared between when this work was written and when it is read.

ISBN: 9798327518001

Printed in the United States of America

I have a gift for you…

Thank you for choosing my book, Practice Game Theory! I would like to show my appreciation for the trust you gave me by giving The Art of Asking Powerful Questions – in the World of Systems to you!

In this booklet you will learn:
-what bounded rationality is,
-how to distinguish event- and behavior-level analysis,
-how to find optimal leverage points,
-and how to ask powerful questions using a systems thinking perspective.

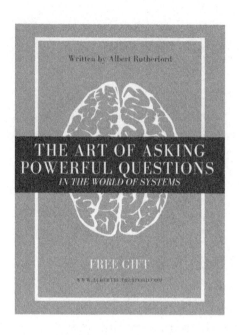

Visit www.albertrutherford.com to claim your gift: The Art of Asking Powerful Questions in the World of Systems

Table of Contents

Chapter 1

The Modern Origin of Statistics - A Bad Cup of Tea

Do you take milk with your coffee? If you do, you probably fill your mug with the hot beverage, then add a dash of milk. Do you ever pour milk or cream in your mug *before* the coffee? According to Food & Beverage Insider, about two thirds of Americans drink coffee every day, and almost half of Americans have a cup of tea every day.[i] And according to the National Coffee Association blog, a little under 30 percent of those coffee drinkers add some sort of milk (be it dairy or dairy-free) to their coffee.[ii] I would hazard a guess that the percentage is higher than that for tea drinkers.

Most of us probably add milk or cream to our coffee or tea rather than adding coffee or tea to our milk or cream. Have you noticed that the order in which you add these liquids changes the taste of what you're drinking? Pouring cold milk into hot liquid changes the flavor of whey proteins; pouring hot liquid into cold milk, by contrast, changes the flavor very little.[iii] And apparently what most of us add-the-milk-after-the-coffee drinkers want is the burnt caramel taste of altered whey proteins.

Believe it or not, that slight taste difference and one woman's ability to identify it were key features in the birth of the modern field of statistical analysis. The general idea of statistics has been around as long as humans (and perhaps other thinking creatures) have, of course. Early humans certainly drew inferences from past experiences; they probably informally collected data on where the best hunting was at what time of year, for example. But the actual field of statistics—the science of collecting and analyzing large sets of data—is a surprisingly recent development.

The main figure behind modern statistics is an English man named Ronald Aylmer Fisher. Fisher was a mathematician and genetics researcher who can be credited with laying the foundation for statistical analysis and experimental design. Despite most of his research being in eugenics, the racially biased and discredited science of "improving" a race's inherited characteristics (that was the foundation of Nazism), his contributions to the field of statistics can't be ignored. After a 1915 paper that established the idea of a correlation coefficient—a number that tells you how closely two phenomena are correlated—his next big breakthrough involved a cup of tea.[iv]

The story goes that, sometime in the early 1920s while Fisher was working at the Rothamsted Experimental Station in England, he offered a colleague named Muriel Bristol a cup of tea. He poured some milk into the cup before he added the tea, and Ms. Bristol refused to drink it. She insisted that tea tastes different if the milk is added before the tea, and that she preferred her tea with the milk added after. Another colleague, a chemist named William Roach, suggested he and Fisher run an experiment to see if Bristol truly could tell the difference between milk added to tea and tea added to milk. They decided to make eight cups of tea—four made with milk first, four with tea first—and give them to Bristol in random order. Sure enough, she could taste the difference between the drinks prepared the two different ways.[v]

As a mathematician, Fisher calculated the mathematical likelihood of Bristol knowing the difference, rather than just guessing and by chance being correct. Fisher figured out that the probability of Bristol just having a streak of luck with eight cups of tea was one in seventy.

This meant it was highly unlikely that she simply guessed. With fewer cups of tea, however, Fisher wouldn't have been so convinced. He figured out that the more cups of tea they provided that she correctly guessed, the more convinced he would be that she could actually taste the difference.[vi] In other words, he discovered the importance of designing an experiment with an appropriate sample size.

We'll talk more about sample size in a later chapter. But for now, back to the tea: Fisher used this story at the beginning of his seminal work on statistics, "Statistical Methods for Research Workers," which he published in 1925. This book has been reprinted many times over the years and is still considered one of the foundational books for modern statistics. Who knew refusing a cup of tea could have such consequences!

If you've gotten this far, chances are you don't have a copy of Fisher's book lying around. You probably have a nagging question about why you should care about statistics. You don't need a college-level class on statistical analysis, but you'd like to know how statistics affect your life. That's what this book is for. The following chapters will give you an idea of how statistics are used in everyday life and how a basic understanding of them can help you make better decisions. You'll learn about why *Barbie* and *Oppenheimer* were such box-office successes, whether you should buy that lottery ticket, and how horror movies could be useful. You'll get a basic understanding of statistical analysis . . . and hopefully be entertained along the way.

Chapter 2

Descriptive Statistics and What We Can Learn From Barbenheimer

In the summer of 2023, two hit movies swept the box offices, becoming a phenomenon known together as Barbenheimer. Barbenheimer—a term most likely coined by film critic David Ehrlich[vii]—was the simultaneous release on July 21st of *Barbie* and *Oppenheimer*, two movies with very different themes but similarly massive budgets and impacts. These two movies dominated the summer, with millions of viewers flocking to cinemas to see *Barbie*, *Oppenheimer*, or even both on the same day (that's a long time to sit still!). Mentions of both movies, as well as outfit pictures of Barbie-goers, dominated social media in July.

If you do a Google search for Barbenheimer memes, you'll find dozens of creative and often hilarious ones that blend the incongruous themes of the two movies. (The

Barbenheimer memes weren't such a hit in Japan, though: Warner Brothers Japan issued an apology for the tone-deaf message of some of the memes, which many people in Japan interpreted as making light of the bombings Japan suffered during World War 2.[viii])

It would be easy to dismiss Barbenheimer as simply a coincidence that helped entertain us during the summer of 2023. But statistics tell us how important this phenomenon actually was to American culture. Analysts credit the two movies with reviving the film industry after three years of lagging sales due to the Covid pandemic. *Variety* even claimed: "The dual release of Greta Gerwig's 'Barbie' and Christopher Nolan's 'Oppenheimer' on July 21 has restored the box office to its pre-COVID glory, and the effects have been felt around the world." One survey of *Barbie*-goers found that nearly one quarter of them hadn't been to a movie in a theater since before the pandemic. *Barbie* brought them to the theaters and prompted many of them to go again: 40 percent of respondents said the experience reminded them how much they loved going to the movies.[ix]

The simultaneous release of the two movies created a synergistic effect, with their popularity feeding off each other and creating a desire in moviegoers to see both. With so many people talking about the two films and so many memes circulating on social media, those who might normally just be interested in one of the movies wondered what the hype was all about. In fact, *The Independent* reported that about six percent of *Oppenheimer* sales could be attributed to *Barbie* tickets being sold out.[x]

Whether or not you scanned social media for the latest Barbenheimer meme, chances are rather good that you saw one or both movies. According to a February 2024 poll about Oscar-nominated movies, nearly one third of Americans had seen *Barbie* and about one fifth had seen *Oppenheimer*. The statistics differ by age group, gender, and even political affiliation, however. More than half of Americans under the age of thirty-five had seen *Barbie*, with a higher percentage of those being women. Those who voted for Trump in 2020 skewed toward *Oppenheimer*, while Biden voters were more likely to have seen *Barbie*.[xi]

Types of Descriptive Statistics

All this data is an example of **descriptive statistics**. Descriptive statistics is exactly what it sounds like: the science of using statistics to describe something that happened. Looking at the data and analyzing it can tell us a great deal about what we have experienced. It helps us make sense of our world, and it can lead us to ask more questions. Why did *Barbie* viewers skew female, younger, and more Democratic, for example? What can that tell us about our society or about the movie? Descriptive statistics also help make a large set of data understandable. They present summaries of events or phenomena with numbers that help us understand what's going on.

The most used descriptive statistics are **measures of central tendency** and **measures of variability**. Measures of central tendency are what you probably learned about in sixth grade (and may have forgotten!): mean, median, and mode, also collectively known as averages. Measures of variability include range and standard deviation, which you may recognize if you took college science classes and had to interpret how well you did compared to the class on an exam.

Measures of central tendency help us make sense of the average or center of a set of data. Measures of variability tell us how widely varying the data is. Think back to that intro psychology exam in college: Maybe you got a ninety-seven and you were thrilled with yourself, quietly gloating that you did so well. Then you saw that the range was only four, meaning the difference between the highest and lowest scores on the exam was only four points. This means most people scored right around a ninety-seven, making you wonder if it's not that you nearly aced a tough exam, but rather that the exam was easy enough that the whole class aced it. Suddenly you don't feel so smart!

On the other hand, if you got a ninety-seven and learned that the range was twenty-three, that means the spread of scores was twenty-three points, so your ninety-seven starts looking pretty good. Without more information, though, we don't know if there was just one person with a score in the seventies or if there were many. The range doesn't tell us anything about how many people got what kind of score.

Let's look at two different scenarios where your ninety-seven means quite different things. Let's say the class has fifty students in it, and forty-nine of them got a seventy-four. Your ninety-seven was the highest score, and you clearly stand out as having done much better on that exam than everyone else. Let's hope this professor grades on a curve! Another scenario is that you got a ninety-seven, one person got a seventy-seven, and forty-eight people got a one hundred. Your ninety-seven is still fairly good, but it doesn't place your score ahead of everyone else's. These are two extremes; the point here is that the range only tells us one piece of information, and it's impossible to know more without using more statistical measures. This is why there are so many ways to measure data sets—each one gives us a small snapshot, but nothing by itself tells a complete story.

Measures of Central Tendency: Mean, Median, and Mode

Let's look at measures of central tendency before coming back to more measures of variability. The three main measures of central tendency people use are **mean**, **median**, and **mode**. The mean is what people usually mean (no pun intended) when they say "average." If you hear that the average number of children per family in the United States is 1.93, that means if you evenly distributed every child in the US to every household, each household would have 1.93 children in it.[xii] We know, of course, that nobody actually has 1.93

children. Instead, this tells us we can safely say it's normal to have two kids, maybe just one. Large households are not the norm in the country—speaking strictly in terms of averages.

The mean can also help us compare data sets easily. Let's look at fertility rates in different countries. The fertility rate is slightly different from the average number of children per household. The fertility rate is defined as "the total number of children that would be born to each woman if she were to live to the end of her child-bearing years and give birth to children in alignment with the prevailing age-specific fertility rates."[xiii] We can think of it as the number of children each woman is expected to have at that point in time. In 2022 the fertility rate in the United States was 1.782.[xiv] In China, by comparison, it was 1.09.

This means that each American woman was expected to have 1.782 children (so one or two), while each Chinese woman was expected to have only 1.09 (so much closer to one). These numbers don't seem all that different— we're talking about a range of .682 (only slightly more than half a child!). But over an entire population, this small difference becomes huge. Imagine most American women have two children, while most Chinese women have one child. Using very rough estimations, America's next generation would be nearly twice as large as China's. No wonder China's president Xi Jinping reportedly worried that his country's rate was so low![xv]

The median is another measure of central tendency that can give us a more complete picture. The median is the exact middle number if the numbers are arranged from least to greatest (or vice versa). The median of a set of data is often used when the mean would be misleading. Let's look at a sample number set. You could imagine that these are the ages of all the children who live on one street:

1, 2, 3, 4, 6, 6, 6, 12, 18

Notice that 6 is listed three times. That's because, to find any of these measures of central tendency, every data point (meaning, in this case, every child on that street) must be listed. So this means there are three six-year-olds on that street—maybe triplets! The median of this set of data—the number exactly in the middle when they're listed in order—is six. That tells us something, but again not everything. It gives us an idea that there are *probably* a bunch of kids under six and a bunch of kids older than six. We don't know how many six-year-olds there are, though. There could be nine six-year-olds on that street, and the median age would still be six. So, again, we get a snapshot but not a full picture of what's going on.

The third measure of central tendency, the mode, gives us another glimpse into the data. The mode is the number that appears most often in your data set; in the case above, the mode is six, since it appears more often than any other number. You could have multiple modes or no mode. Imagine, for example, that there were also eleven-year-old triplets; in that case, the modes would be six and eleven. If there were no repeat ages—every child on the street was a unique age—then there wouldn't be a mode.

Too Many Fish

One of my favorite data sets to talk about comes from a teacher friend of mine. She was teaching a small class of thirteen elementary school students, and she asked them how many pets they each had at home, thinking this would make a nice data set to work with. It turned out to be even more interesting than she had predicted. Most students answered zero, one, or two, but one precocious student counted all her fish and concluded she had seventeen pets. Here's how the survey data looked:

Number of pets	Tally
0	2
1	5
2	3
3	2
17	1

This set of data is a great example of why we need all three measures of center—as well as the range, ideally—to get an accurate picture of what's going on. For this set, the **median** (remember, that's the number in the middle when we line up every data point from least to greatest) is 1. Someone might conclude that a handful of students have fewer than one pet and a handful have more than one pet. They'd be correct . . . but they'd be missing the fact that that one student had answered seventeen. The **mode**, or the most common answer, is also 1. The **mean**, however, is 2.62.

Remember that when most people say "average," they're referring to the mean. If that teacher had reported that the average number of pets owned by students in her class was 2.62, you might have concluded that most kids in that class had two or three pets. The mean isn't *wrong*, but it's misleading on its own. In that class, more students had zero or one pet (2+5=7) than two or three pets (3+2=5). That 17 skewed the average!

This same thing happens when we look at incomes in the US, which are highly stratified. According to the federal reserve, the top 1 percent of households in the US own more than 30 percent of the wealth.[xvi] If we found the "average" (mean) amount of wealth owned by people in the United States, that richest 1 percent would pull the average up, and the resulting measure would be misleading. In fact, according to US Census data, the estimated mean income in 2022 (adjusted for inflation) was $105,555, while the median was just $74,755.[xvii] This is why wealth is usually described by the median, since that gives us a better picture of the typical American family. The more unbalanced the data set is, the less useful the mean is, since a concentration at the top or the bottom pulls the mean in that direction.

Measures of center can be useful, but even using all three of them doesn't give you a complete picture. Mean, median, and mode provide a quick snapshot of what is going on with a data set, but you would need to look at all the data (and more sophisticated measures) to get a more complete picture. There's a famous phrase among data scientists that illustrates the limitations of measures of center: "If your head is in the oven and your feet are in the freezer, on average, you feel just fine."[xviii]

Limitations

Measures of center also don't necessarily tell you anything about what is going to happen; they don't help you make predictions, but rather describe what has already happened. If we look back at the Barbenheimer statistics quoted earlier, we'd probably guess that *Barbie* had cleaned up at the Oscars. More people saw it than saw *Oppenheimer*, and it grossed more than $1.4 billion, where *Oppenheimer* grossed a little under $1 billion.[xix] [xx] *Barbie*'s feminist message seemed perfectly timed for the summer of 2023. Yet many fans were shocked when *Oppenheimer* received thirteen nominations to *Barbie*'s eight. Fans were particularly upset that Greta Gerwig, who co-wrote and directed *Barbie*, didn't get nominated for Best Director, and that Margot Robbie, who played Barbie, wasn't nominated for Best Actress. Meanwhile Ryan Gosling, portrayer of Ken, was nominated for Best Supporting Actor. Memes abounded, with some declaring that Barbie getting snubbed while Ken got recognized was "basically the plot of the movie." The *LA Times* ran an opinion piece by Mary McNamara with the headline "Shocking Oscar snubs for *Barbie*'s Greta Gerwig and Margot Robbie just prove the movie's point."[xxi]

None of this is to say that *Oppenheimer*'s awards (including Best Picture, Best Director, and Best Actor) weren't well deserved. What we can learn from this is that statistics—particularly descriptive statistics—can be interesting and fun to learn about, but they can't predict the future. *Barbie*'s performance in the box office couldn't tell us what the Academy would decide. There is a field of statistics, however, that can give us more insight into human behavior, allowing us to make predictions and inferences. That's what you'll learn about in the next chapter.

Chapter 3

Inferential Statistics and Why Horror Fans Are More Ready for an Apocalypse

I grew up with a sibling who loved fantasy books and movies. She was into superheroes, apocalypse scenarios, and wild imaginary creatures. I was the realist, more interested in fiction and non-fiction that reflected on the world around me. We couldn't understand each other.

"How can you not like fantasy?" she would say.

"How can *you* spend your time in imaginary worlds?" I would reply. The bickering was constant until, as adults, we agreed to disagree.

It turns out my sister's love of the imaginary might have made her more prepared for something very real: the Covid-19 pandemic. A team of psychologists conducted research showing that fans of certain genres may have been more prepared for the psychological effects of the pandemic. Let's take a minute to think back to the spring of 2020, the early days of the pandemic. In the United States, people were urged to stay home (not mandated to, as they were in many other countries); stores, offices, and schools shut down; hospitals in some parts of the country turned away ambulances, and the news was dominated by how many people had died from Covid that week. Experts did not know yet how exactly the virus spread (droplets? Airborne particles? Germs on grocery bags? Suddenly we all became experts in germ theory).

Highways and grocery shelves sat empty as people hunkered down, afraid to be near others, unsure of what the future would hold. It's hard to recall the intensity of it now, but the virus called into question the systems our lives were built on; it wouldn't have been far-fetched to wonder if this virus would cause the breakdown of civilization.

Colton Scrivner, a graduate student in human development and biology who was interested in the psychology of horror, wondered if some people were better prepared for the psychological effects of the pandemic than others. He reached out to several researchers, and together they devised a survey of three hundred people that looked at what kinds of films they enjoyed and gauged their psychological reactions to the pandemic. According to John Johnson, one of the researchers on the project, "After factoring out personality influences . . . we found that the more movies about zombies, alien invasions and apocalyptic pandemics people had seen prior to COVID-19, the better they dealt with the actual, current pandemic. These kinds of movies apparently serve as mental rehearsal for actual events."[xxii]

This fascinating survey is an example of inferential statistics, a field that uses numbers to make inferences and predictions about life and behavior. Descriptive statistics is all about analyzing a data set to describe something; inferential statistics involves creating a sample data set and drawing inferences. So what is a sample set, how do researchers create one, and what kinds of information can they infer?

The Importance of Sampling

Imagine that you wanted to find out something about a large population. Let's say you were wondering if most people in the

United States prefer wearing mittens or gloves when it is cold out. It would be pretty much impossible for you to survey every single person in the country about that. To make things a little easier for yourself, you would choose a *sample*, or a smaller set of the population that is representative of the whole. That second part—representative of the whole—is really important and also often difficult. Why? If your sample isn't representative of the entire population, you won't be able to use it to draw accurate inferences.

Imagine that, for your sample set in the survey about mittens versus gloves, you go to a playground and ask everyone there which they prefer. Surprisingly to you, ninety percent of survey respondents answer that they prefer mittens. You also may notice, however, that ninety percent of survey respondents are children under the age of five. It's safe to say that most young children wear mittens because they're easier for parents to put on them, not because they've tried both and decided mittens better fit their lifestyle. It would be inaccurate to then infer that ninety percent of the entire population of the US also prefers mittens, because your sample—mostly children—isn't representative of the entire US population, which is only about twenty-six percent children ages 0–4.[xxiii]

On the other hand, if you surveyed a line of taxi drivers waiting at an airport, your data would also be unreliable. Taxi drivers must handle steering wheels and luggage all day; it would be harder to do that in thick fuzzy mittens than in nice driving gloves. To get answers that you could reliably draw inferences from, your sample—the group of people you survey—would have to be proportional to the entire population of the US. Each subgroup that you identify—children, adults, taxi drivers, Floridians, for example—would have to exist in the same proportions that they do in the entire population.

Creating a sample is one of the hardest and most important steps in gathering data. Over the years, plenty of studies have been published that had to be retracted because somebody figured out there was a problem with the sample. Even excellently run studies contain sampling error, which is the unavoidable difference between the sample and the larger population. A researcher's goal is to minimize sampling error.

One famously wrong survey occurred in the run-up to the 1936 election. Writers at the magazine *Literary Digest* used car registrations, telephone numbers, and country club memberships to survey people about whom they were going to vote for: the Democratic candidate, Franklin D. Roosevelt, or the Republican candidate, Alfred Landon. Only about 2.4 million of the 10 million people polled responded. From those responses, the *Digest* predicted Landon to win by a margin of 57 percent to 43 percent and would carry thirty-two states. It turns out Roosevelt won 62 percent to 37 percent, carrying all but two states.

There were two main problems with the sample: First, the majority of the identified sample did not respond, meaning that those who did respond were the ones who felt more passionate about responding. It was a self-selected group. Perhaps they were more adamant about voting than the non-responders were, or perhaps they leaned Republican for some reason. The other problem with the sample is that it was biased toward wealthier people (those who owned cars or telephones or belonged to a country club). This election was during the Great Depression, and FDR campaigned as a populist who would bring relief to the poor.[xxiv]

A more recent example that you may remember was in the 2016 election. Leading up to Election Day, nearly every poll showed Hillary Clinton winning by a large margin, with some even saying she had a 99 percent chance of winning. Yet she lost to Donald Trump, including in Pennsylvania and Wisconsin, where she was heavily favored to win. So what happened? How did political researchers get it so wrong?

Many are still debating this (and trying not to make the same mistake in upcoming elections). Most of the theories of what happened relate to the sample. One theory is that there was a "non-response bias" similar to that in the 1936 election: The people who didn't respond to the polls were the ones who primarily supported Trump. There may also have been a lack of enthusiasm among the identified "voters" in the survey, meaning many people may have responded that they supported Clinton but didn't actually vote on Election Day. Trump also had a lot of support from both Hispanic Americans and poorer Americans, both of whom are notoriously harder to reach with polls.[xxv]

Making Inferences

These two examples show us how critical the sample is in inferential statistics, and how, even with modern technology, sampling can get things wrong. This is why the field is called *inferential* statistics: We can make inferences based on data, but we can't be 100 percent sure our predictions will be correct. Fortunately, every survey that turns out to have been wrong gives statisticians more information to work with the next time, more potential pitfalls to be aware of in the collection of data.

Inferential statistics are also used in market research. If you've ever been asked to participate in a study or a poll, you were most likely identified as part of a sample set. Market research firms' existence is based on inferential statistics and predictions. Researchers will test out a hypothesis (say, a new commercial or logo) on a sample that is supposed to be representative of the entire population and then make inferences based on the sample's responses. If the sample responds positively to, for example, the new jingle for a brand of dog food, you might hear the jingle on TV the following year.

The healthcare industry relies on inferential statistics as well. Drug companies use outcomes from samples—say, the percentage of people in a group who responded favorably to a certain drug—to decide whether to market it to the larger population. Insurance companies use data from sample sets to predict outcomes, and these predictions guide costs and decisions about coverage. Much of what seems unfair or arbitrary on an individual level is based on inferential statistics, which cannot accurately predict one person's health outcomes.

Let's take a deeper look at how these healthcare decisions are made. Say, for example, you want to try a new medication for acne that your friend, who has tried many different medications to treat acne, has recommended. Your doctor prescribes it to you, but insurance won't cover it because they want you to try another less expensive medication first. Although they might be making decisions based on profit, they might also have information showing that most people respond to the cheaper medication. There is no way for them to know how you as an individual will respond to each medication, but they are using the data they have to predict just that—and to potentially save money in the long run. Inferential statistics help people identify trends and make predictions that aren't necessarily correct for each individual.

Predicting Your Movie Choices

Finally, inferential statistics probably plays a massive role in your life that you're not even aware of. If you use streaming platforms to watch your favorite shows—Netflix, Hulu, Amazon Prime, or another—you've probably noticed their personalized recommendations. These recommendations are based on inferential statistics—analyses of users similar to you. Streaming platforms take user information and offer you what shows or movies they *think* you will like. Nowadays, you won't find a team of mathematicians looking at your personal data and trying to predict your exact behavior, since artificial intelligence and computer programming can do most of the work. But way back in the early- to mid-aughts, teams of programmers did have to crunch numbers to try to figure out what viewers might like.

In 2006, when streaming platforms were in their infancy (YouTube launched in 2005), companies were just starting to think about how they could better serve—and profit from—individuals' viewing habits. The need for an innovative way to predict people's preferences was so great that Netflix launched The Netflix Prize, a competition to improve their prediction system by 10 percent. This was back when Netflix was a DVD-by-mail company without streaming. CEO Reed Hastings knew that Netflix's credibility rested in part on it seeming to know what its customers wanted, so he announced a one million dollar prize for whoever could improve their prediction accuracy by ten percent. Data scientists, big tech companies, professors, and even college students took the published data and began eagerly crunching numbers.[xxvi]

Although nobody crossed that threshold of a ten percent improved recommendation system until 2009, the prize spurred great advances in data mining and statistical modeling. Those working to crack the ten percent line enthusiastically shared ideas and formulas on internet forums, often working in collaboration rather than competition. As *Thrillist* put it, "The forums . . . were a hotbed of problem-solving, discussion, and joyful discovery. Imagine a digital summer camp for researchers."[xxvii] It would be hard to overstate the impact this early work had on the algorithms streaming companies now use. The personalized recommendations you get when you open Netflix, Hulu, or any other streaming service now are the result of years of improving upon the number crunching that Netflix inspired.

It's not just streaming companies that rely on data analysis and inferences about their users. Anytime you use the internet, you see ads that are specifically targeted to you. Have a chat with your partner about needing to buy new glasses, and you'll start seeing ads for glasses on social media. It's (probably) not that your computer or phone are listening to you, but rather that big tech companies are constantly gathering and analyzing data from you and users like you to predict what you might want. They know, based on your usage, what your interests are, where you live, what time of day you usually leave the house, and all sorts of other details about you; they know the same for all the people you interact with. They probably know that you searched the internet for "eye doctors" recently but haven't searched for new glasses in a few years. Maybe they even know that your partner recently bought a pair of glasses online. They have so much data that they can predict, with remarkable accuracy sometimes, our next move.

Whether or not you're aware of it, inferential statistics are part of your life. If you have a phone, a computer, a television, or any other modern device, you produce data that can be analyzed. That analysis leads to inferences, which lead to predictions about your behavior, which lead to marketing, which leads to purchasing, which leads to even more data. Humans (with the help of computers) have gotten so good at using data that we don't even notice how much the use of inferential statistics impacts our lives.

Chapter 4

Probability and Your Chance of Winning a Million Dollars

If you're a game-show watcher, you've probably wondered how well you'd do as a contestant on your favorite show. Maybe you're the friend in the group who knows all the answers to *Jeopardy*, or maybe you're the person confidently guessing wrong each time. Have you ever calculated the actual probability of you winning? The odds are quite slim!

Let's look at the show *Who Wants to Be a Millionaire*, a game show that started in 1998 and was incredibly popular for about two decades. In case you're unfamiliar with it, contestants get the opportunity to answer fifteen multiple-choice questions of increasing difficulty, with an ever-increasing monetary reward. If they answer all fifteen correctly, they win one million dollars. Between 1998 and 2020, only twelve players in the United States version won the top prize. The first five questions are easy (sometimes ridiculously so!), designed to help the players win a bit of money and relax. Then they start getting harder. In the original version, players have three lifelines they can use if they don't know the answer to a question: phone a friend (a preselected friend who is waiting to receive the call), ask the audience, or 50/50, which removes two incorrect answer choices, leaving two behind. As soon as the player answers one question incorrectly, the game is over and the player leaves with an amount of money determined by what tier of question they were on.

David Patrick, a 1999 contestant on the show (who left with $64,000, in case you're curious), wrote an entry on the website The Art of Problem-Solving that explored the probability of a random person winning a million dollars on the show. Patrick walks us through the possibilities: Maybe you randomly guess on all fifteen questions because you don't know any of the answers. That gives you a one in one billion chance of winning the million-dollar prize. Not so great. If you know the answers to the first five, as most people do, you only have to randomly guess on ten questions, and now your odds of winning are one in a million. Not too bad! But still not great. As he puts it, "If you played WWTBAM every thirty minutes, twenty-four-hours-a-day, it would 'only' take you fifty-seven years, on average, to win the million." Finally, Patrick calculates that if you get the first ten correct, as he did, randomly guessing on only the last five, you have a one in one thousand chance of winning. He then works in the lifelines (assuming you haven't used any of them yet) and figures out that you have a one in twenty chance of winning. The odds are still against you, but not terribly so. If you can get through those first ten without using any of your lifelines, you have a decent shot at a million dollars![xxviii]

The probability of something happening—like winning a million dollars on a game show—is found by dividing the number of favorable outcomes by the total possible outcomes. For WWTBAM, each question has four answer choices, so the probability of getting each question right is one in four (one favorable outcome, or correct answer choice, divided by four possible outcomes, or total answer choices). So then why isn't the probability of winning a million dollars one in four? For multiple correct answers in a row, we need to calculate compound probability, or the odds that something (a correct answer) will occur more than once. It's like flipping a coin:

Each time you flip it, there is a fifty-fifty chance of it landing on heads, but there is a much smaller chance of it landing on heads ten times in a row (a little less than one in a thousand!).

Luck and the Lottery

Let's use dice to examine probability more. People talk about "lucky sevens" in dice, and many people claim seven as their lucky number. But why would seven be any luckier than any other number? What makes seven so special? If you look at possible outcomes from rolling two dice, you can see that seven is more likely than any other number to appear. These are all the possible rolls of two dice, with the number in red representing one die (let's say Die A) and the number in blue representing the other (Die B):

Sum	Ways to roll that sum
0	Not possible
1	Not possible
2	1+1
3	1+2 2+1
4	1+3 2+2 3+1
5	1+4 2+3 3+2 4+1
6	1+5 2+4 3+3 4+2 5+1
7	1+6 2+5 3+4 4+3 5+2 6+1
8	2+6 3+5 4+4 5+3 6+2

9	3+6 4+5 5+4 6+3
10	4+6 5+5 6+4
11	5+6 6+5
12	6+6

The total possible outcomes—every single way the two dice could land—is thirty-six. That means the denominator of our fraction will always be thirty-six. For the numerator, we look at the number of favorable outcomes, or outcomes we are looking for. Let's say we're trying to figure out the probability of rolling a four. There are three possible ways to get a four.

Three divided by thirty-six is one in twelve, or .08. Probabilities are usually given as percents, so we can say there is an 8 percent chance of rolling a four. Similar calculations yield a one in thirty-six, or about 3 percent, chance of rolling a two or a twelve. There are more ways (six) to make seven than any other number in the table, so the probability of rolling a seven is one in six, or nearly seventeen percent. It turns out sevens aren't necessarily "lucky," but just mathematically more likely.

Speaking of luck, millions of people every day try their hand at the lottery. It may be fun to dream about winning and being able to afford a beach house, college for your kids and grandkids, and early retirement, but pretty much everyone agrees that playing the lottery isn't a worthwhile investment. Every lottery game has different odds of winning, depending on how many combinations of numbers are possible. According to Investopedia, the odds of winning any payout in Powerball are one in 24.9.[xxix] That doesn't seem too outrageous, right? Maybe you're thinking it is worth playing!

That's not the whole picture, though. Powerball isn't an all-or-nothing game. If you win, it turns out you have excellent odds (more than nine in ten, or above 90 percent) of winning just $4. The lowest price of a Powerball ticket is $2, so in essence you have a *very* slim chance of profiting any more than $2. In fact, the chances of you winning the jackpot in Powerball are one in 292.2 million. In the language of probability, that is *highly unlikely*. Put into perspective, you are much more likely to be struck by lightning in a given year than to win the Powerball jackpot.[xxx]

Weather Forecasts

Probability also plays a key role in weather forecasting. All weather forecasts are probabilistic, meaning they are based on predictions about what will probably, but not definitely, happen given the existing conditions. Depending on where you live, you've likely experienced a forecast that was overblown or completely missed. We've seen headlines like "Massive winter storm coming today!" that lead to empty store shelves and closed schools, only to have just a dusting of snow fall.

If you experienced that (and your kids stayed home from school), you probably derided your local weather forecaster: How could they get it so wrong? We've all seen the other extreme as well—hurricanes that hit in a different place than they were predicted to, or massive storms that seemed to come out of nowhere, again leading us to question our forecasters' abilities.

You may have even heard stories of weather forecasters who famously got their forecasts wrong. Perhaps you've heard the story of Michael Fish, the BBC news weatherman who will never live down his words on October 15th of 1987, shortly before Britain's "Great Storm" hit. "Earlier on today," he told viewers that day, "a woman rang the BBC and said she heard there was a hurricane on the way . . . Well, if you're watching, don't worry, there isn't!" Technically, he was right: The storm was a cyclone, not a hurricane. But it caused eighteen deaths and widespread damage across the United Kingdom, with some calling it the strongest storm to hit the area in three hundred years. Poor Michael Fish's life was miserable after that (partly because he refused to admit he was wrong). Newspaper headlines the day after reveal how blindsided people felt:[xxxi]

Daily Mail

SATURDAY, OCTOBER 17, 1987   20p

68 PAGES TODAY

At least 17 dead, hundreds injured, homes wrecked, thousands can't get to work and Britain's storm bill could reach £1 billion

WHY WEREN'T WE WARNED?

Daily Mail Reporters

THOUSANDS of families devastated by Britain's worst weather disaster for nearly 300 years yesterday were left asking: Why was there no warning?

Only hours before the hurricane swept across southern Britain at more than 100 mph, the experts were predicting no more than 'rather strong winds.'

BBC weatherman Michael Fish told his viewers: 'A woman rang to say she'd heard there was a hurricane on the way. Well don't worry, there isn't.'

Hours later, at least 17 people lay dead and the country was counting the massive cost of the damage and disruption — about £1 billion.

Tragedies

As the AA said: 'If we had been able to advise people earlier that they should not drive or at least should seek out for obstacles in the road, perhaps some of those tragedies could have been avoided.'

So what exactly did go wrong?

The weather forecasters blamed a computer nicknamed Beastie — part of a £6 million high-tech complex backed up by two satellites and 2,400 staff in an organisation paid £75 million a year by the Ministry of Defence to get it right.

As the hurricane headed for Britain from the Bay of Biscay, the computer estimated wind speeds of around 80mph.

Martin Morley a senior forecaster at the London Weather Centre, said 'There's obviously a fault in Beastie's computer programme.'

When the storm hit Bracknell (the Met

Turn to Page 5, Col.4

Victim of the hurricane

CRUSHED: Firemen recover a body from a car wrecked when an uprooted tree fell onto a road at Petersfield, Hampshire

Cancer test for Nancy Reagan

From Mail Correspondent in Washington

PRESIDENT Reagan's wife Nancy is to have tests for suspected breast cancer today.

If they prove positive, her left breast will be removed immediately.

Mr and Mrs Reagan, who have been married 35 years, made the decision to proceed with a mastectomy, if necessary, after talking together and with doctors on Friday.

A suspicious lump was discovered when the 66-year-old

Mrs Reagan: Check

First Lady had a routine check earlier in the week.

White House spokesman Marlin Fitzwater said: Generally, she feels very positive about it. She made the comment, when this was first discovered: 'I guess it's my turn.'

Mrs Reagan has been credited with being the power behind the 76-year-old President. They have a very close and romantic marriage. He calls her 'Mommy,' while she is fiercely protective towards him.

INSIDE: Hot Gossip 7, Medical Notebook 8, World Wide 10, Femail 12,13, TV 21-24, Home Front 26, Skiing 28,29, Gardening 30,31, Supermatch 32, City 36,37, Sport 39-44

Luckily, weather forecasts have significantly improved since 1987, but they are still *predictions* based on what forecasters, aided by computer models, think will most likely happen.

Let's look more closely at the kind of forecast we see daily: the chance of precipitation. You may look at the weather forecast for your town and see that there is an 80 percent chance of rain today. But what exactly does that mean? Does it mean that eighty percent of your town will see rain? Or that it will rain for 80 percent of the day? For most (but not all[1]) forecasters, it doesn't mean either of those.

Precipitation forecasts, or PoPs (probability of precipitation), as they're known in the industry, are one forecaster's guess about one point in your area seeing precipitation (defined as greater than .01 inches of rain) that day.[xxxii] If your weather app says there is an 80 percent chance of rain, that means that <u>somewhere in your area </u>will *probably* (80

---

[1] Some forecasters do use chance of rain to represent the percentage of an area that will most likely get rain. In this case, saying an 80% chance of rain would mean that they expect 80% of the local area to get rain that day. Forecasters who use this definition are supposed to disclose that they are defining chance of rain differently than most do.

percent likely) see rain that day. If it doesn't rain on your house, that doesn't mean the forecast was wrong; remember there was still a 20 percent chance that there would be no rain. It's also possible that it rained two hundred yards down the road.

When you're looking at weather forecasts, it's helpful to keep in mind some basic terminology around probabilities. When students learn about probability in school, they usually learn about it as a continuum, where 0 percent is impossible and 100 percent is certain.

This simple scale can help you plan your day. If the chance of rain is less than 50 percent, you might want to water your garden. If it's more than 50 percent, maybe hold off (and carry an umbrella with you to work). Either way, though, remember that even a 99 percent chance of rain doesn't mean it will definitely rain exactly where you are that day—try to go easy on your weather forecasters!

Unfortunately for them, two top Hungarian meteorologists were fired in 2022 when it didn't rain. In August of 2022, Hungary's national meteorological service predicted severe storms for the country's national holiday, Saint Stephen's Day. Based on the forecast, the government decided to postpone celebratory fireworks. When it didn't rain, people were outraged, and the head of the weather service, as well as her deputy, were fired. The Hungarian government claimed that these two were about to be fired anyway, but the story stands that the two lost their jobs because it didn't rain.[xxxiii]

Calculating Probability for Profit

Probability doesn't just come into play in weather forecasts and rolling dice. Some people have made massive amounts of money based on knowing how to calculate probabilities. Have you ever played cards with a card counter? Or are you one yourself? You know the type: those who analyze and keep track of every move in a card game, mentally tallying which cards have been played and which ones are left to play. Card counting can be as simple as keeping track of the face cards in a game of Go Fish, or as complicated as the

MIT Blackjack team that trained students in the 1990s to beat casinos. It can involve not just knowing which cards are left to play, but the probabilities of certain cards appearing. Once you know those probabilities, you can bet large sums of money and beat the casino . . . until they throw you out, that is.

That's what happened to the team from MIT. While card counting isn't illegal, casinos don't like it because it makes them lose money. The saying is that the house always wins, but with a dedicated card counter, the house can lose. So who were these MIT students and how did they manage to beat the house?

The MIT Blackjack team formed in the early 1990s as a group of students who were good at math—of course—and interested in gambling. Advised by a successful card counter named Bill Kaplan (who had postponed his college experience at Harvard to go win money in Vegas), the team of students learned how to beat the odds at Blackjack by keeping track of the cards that had been played. This was a business venture for Kaplan, and a quite lucrative activity for many of the students, as they joined the high rollers clubs at casinos across the country. One by one, though, the students got kicked out of casinos or barred from playing Blackjack at those casinos. A private investigator eventually realized that they all came from MIT, and the game was over, so to speak. The team folded and Kaplan moved on to other ventures, though some players continued to make their money as Blackjack champs.[xxxiv] But the story lives on: A bunch of data nerds won hundreds of thousands of dollars by using what they knew about probability.

Chapter 5

Genetics and the Likelihood of Redheads

Let's look at another field where probability is used all the time: genetics. If you took high school biology, you may remember Punnett squares. To a fourteen-year-old, Punnett squares seem like magical predictors that lend a glimpse into what geneticists do. In reality, Punnett squares are a visual tool to represent some standard probability calculations.

If you are a biological parent, you likely put some thought into what your child would look like before they came out of the womb. Will the baby have my curly brown hair? Will he or she have my wife's green eyes? Will the baby be long and lean, like my side of the family, or on the shorter side, like my wife's family? How about my weird ability to roll my tongue—will the baby get that? Sometimes the kids come out looking just like you expected.

Sometimes, though, they don't; they have some trait that nobody on either side of the family had except for your great aunt Edna.

To understand more about genetics, we must delve deeper into probability. In the last chapter, we looked at the probability of an event occurring. That's a simple calculation: the number of favorable outcomes divided by the number of total possible outcomes. Now let's look at compound probability. That means we want to figure out the likelihood of *two* independent events happening. There's a handy rule to help us here: the product rule.

The product rule tells us that, to calculate the probability of two independent events both happening, we multiply their two probabilities. Let's say we want to figure out how likely it is that a coin lands on heads two times in a row. For each flip, the probability of it landing on heads is ½. For the probability of it landing on heads one time AND a second time, we multiply ½ by itself (for each flip) and get ¼. There is a one in four possibility (or 25 percent) that a coin will land on heads twice in a row.

Punnett Squares

Now for some basics on genetics: Every person inherits copies of genes from two biological parents. These genes determine all sorts of traits—everything that makes up an individual, in essence. Let's call these two genes A and a, meaning two different versions (alleles) of the same gene, one from the mother and one from the father. In genetics, the dominant allele—the one that appears in the child—is represented with a capital letter, and the recessive allele—the one that the child carries but that doesn't show up—is represented with a lowercase letter. For example, let's imagine a person with black hair who also inherited a recessive gene for blond hair. This person is said to be heterozygous, meaning they inherited two *different* alleles (hence the hetero- prefix) for a trait. We'll call the dominant gene that produces black hair uppercase A, and the recessive gene that produces blonde hair lowercase a. This is Parent 1 in the diagram below:

Parent 1 →	A	a

Parent 1 has a child with another individual, Parent 2, who also happens to have black hair and a recessive gene for blond hair. This person is represented by the left-hand column of the diagram:

Parent 1 → Parent 2 ↓	A	a
A		
a		

Since every child gets alleles from both parents, we complete the table with the possible combinations of alleles that their children could get from them:

Parent 1 → Parent 2 ↓	A	a
A	AA	Aa
a	Aa	aa

Each of the squares in the table represents the probability that the child will have that combination of alleles. Remember that the dominant allele—represented by the capital A—represents black hair, and if it appears in the square, the child will present with that trait. So that means there is a three in four chance, or 75 percent probability, that the child will have black hair, and—maybe surprisingly—only a one in four chance (25 percent) that the child will have blond hair.

This might seem second-nature to you. If you and your partner both have black hair, it makes sense that your child will probably have black hair. But let's look at the chances of two parents having a red-headed child. Redheads are notoriously rare, but why? Here's a handy visual from the website Let's Talk Science of the possible Punnett squares for these two people[xxxv]:

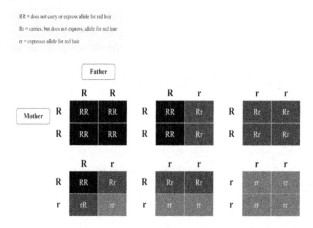

RR = does not carry or express allele for red hair
Rr = carries, but does not express, allele for red hair
rr = expresses allele for red hair

You can see that there are many more ways for the child *not* to have red hair than there are for the child to have red hair. Even if one parent is a redhead, the other parent has to be carrying a gene for red hair for the possibility of it to express itself in the child. If just one of you says, "My great-grandmother had red hair; I wonder if our kid will," science can pretty much guarantee that your kid will not have red hair. If only one parent has red hair and the other one carries the gene—let's say their mother and brother have red hair— there is still only a fifty-fifty chance that the child will have red hair. The only way you can be sure your child will have red hair is if both parents have red hair.

Mendelian Genetics

Those small Punnett squares may have been the extent of your high school biology education. But the idea of a Punnett square—a visual representation of probabilities—goes far beyond two heterozygotes. The biologist Gregor Mandel, known as the father of modern genetics, extensively studied peas in the nineteenth century to figure out how dominant and recessive traits work. In particular, he studied dihybrid crosses—what happens when two organisms with two different traits reproduce. The two traits he examined were color (whether the peas were green or yellow) and wrinkliness (whether they were smooth or wrinkly). A larger Punnett square illustrates his findings[xxxvi]:

Dihybrid Cross in Pea Plant

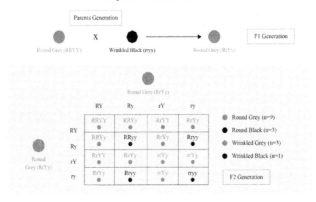

We can see that crossing a round yellow pea with a wrinkled green pea turns out to have only a one in sixteen chance that the offspring will be wrinkled and green.

Genetic Testing

You may be thinking that's enough of a science lesson for now, and who really cares about peas anyway. The basic idea of Mendelian genetics is used all the time by biologists and geneticists to predict risks of different diseases. Certain diseases are much more common in particular races or ethnicities. For example, sickle cell anemia is much more common among people of sub-Saharan African, Middle Eastern, Asian, or South American descent. According to the National Institute of Health in the United States, "about 1 in every 365 Black or African American babies is born with SCA. About 1 in every 13 are born with SCT (sickle cell trait, meaning they carry the gene but have less severe disease). In contrast, only 1 in 333 white babies is born with SCT."[xxxvii]

There are also many diseases that are more common among people of Jewish descent. Remember that parents don't necessarily need to have the disease to be a carrier of it. Most geneticists and obstetricians recommend to their Jewish patients—particularly those with Ashkenazi heritage—that they get a panel of genetic testing done, commonly known as the "Jewish panel."[xxxviii] This panel can tell them if one or both parents are carriers for certain diseases and the likelihood of their children presenting with each of these diseases.

Let's look at Tay-Sachs disease, a truly terrible neurodegenerative disease that usually takes its victim's life by the age of five. This disease, like several others, is much more prevalent in those of Ashkenazi Jewish or French-Canadian descent.[2] Although the disease is rare, it still behooves future parents to find out if they are carriers of the disease. Why subject themselves to that? Because the likelihood of the child having it is so high and the disease so terrible that future parents would probably want to be fully informed. For Tay-Sachs to present, both parents need to be carriers. Let's make a Punnett square for this scenario, where both parents are carriers but not presenting with the disease. We can say each of their genes is represented by Tt—the dominant non-altered gene plus the recessive altered gene.

---

[2] Tay-Sachs is not the only disease that is more common in these two specific populations. Information on why these two populations overlap in this way is scarce, but it's possible that French settlers in Canada also had Jewish ancestry.

Parent 1 → Parent 2 ↓	T	t
T	TT	Tt
t	Tt	tt

From the square, we can see that there is a one in four chance (the tt at the bottom right) that the child will have Tay-Sachs disease. That's a pretty high chance for something so awful. There is also a two in four (or 50 percent) chance that the child will be a carrier for the disease, meaning that child will likely want their future partner to get tested before they someday have children.[xxxix] This likelihood is the same for each child that this couple has. It doesn't mean that, if they have four children, one of them *will* have Tay-Sachs and two others *will* be carriers, but it means that each pregnancy independently carries this risk.

To leave this chapter on a lighter note: Remember that knowledge is power. The more you know about genetic risks of different diseases, the more informed your decisions will be and the better prepared you will be to handle life's challenges. You'll also be better able to explain why your child doesn't have red hair, despite your great aunt Edna being a flaming redhead.

Chapter 6

Data Analysis and Interpretation - Making the Best Baseball Team

Have you seen the 2011 movie *Moneyball*? Or read Michael Lewis's 2004 book on which the movie is based? If so, I'd hazard a guess that you're either a baseball fan or a Brad Pitt fan. When most casual observers think of baseball, they might picture long afternoons in sunny stands, eating crackerjacks, stretches of inactivity followed by bursts of excitement when someone hits a home run. We think of those power hitters and ace pitchers, the ones who draw a crowd and inspire awe with their strength and athleticism. What we don't usually think of is a high-level data analyst on the team.

Data analysts have played a key role in baseball since 2002, when a revolutionary approach by the Oakland A's proved how powerful data analysis could be. As described in *Moneyball*, the story of the Oakland A's goes somewhat like this: In the late 1990s, the A's had a terrible record. New general manager Billy Beane wanted to turn that around, particularly after he lost three top players in 2001. He turned to a colleague named Paul DePodesta, a scout with a degree in economics from Harvard. DePodesta and Beane began combing through data to try to figure out what actually helped them win games. Was it the big hitters? The ace closer? Or was it something else that people might be overlooking?

Beane and DePodesta used a form of data analysis called Sabermetrics, created by Bill James in 1980. James defined it as "the search for objective knowledge about baseball."[xl] This approach had been around for decades, but few people in baseball were using it; instead, scouts and managers tended to rely on what fans notice: the grand-slam hitter, the pitcher who strikes out six batters in a row—the ones who grab your attention. Sabermetrics is the practice of taking a deeper look at the statistics and running predictive models to see what—and who—can help you actually win a game.

In their analyses, Beane and DePodesta found that oft-overlooked statistics, including on-base percentage (the percentage of time a specific batter makes it onto the bases, whether that is from a hit or a walk), were much more predictive of a team's success than the statistics most scouts and managers cared about, which included RBIs, batting averages, and home runs. The A's had seven first-round draft picks for the 2002 season. Beane surprised other managers and scouts by picking college athlete Nick Swisher in the first round.[xli] Indeed, all of his first-round picks went against what traditional baseball scouts advised: they weren't the sought-after players with the highest averages or number of RBIs. They weren't players that teams with higher budgets, like the New York Yankees, were trying to sign. The A's worked with a small budget of just $40 million (compared to the Yankees' $120 billion) to put together a team that data, not necessarily instinct, told them would do well.[xlii]

By the end of the season, they had the winningest record in the Major Leagues and had broken the American League's nineteen-game winning streak set by the 1947 Yankees. The A's performance that season revolutionized baseball. Teams now use Sabermetrics to guide nearly every aspect of the game—what players to sign, what kind of swing a player should practice to improve their on-base percentage, and when to bring in which pitcher based on what batters are due up.[xliii] Teams now employ high-level data analysts to help managers and coaches make these kinds of decisions.

Big Data and Its Many Uses

If big data—the collection and analysis of a constant stream of data points—can revolutionize the game of baseball, what else can it do?

Data is ubiquitous. What you may think of as everyday life—a few clicks on the internet, a grocery-shopping trip, a Sunday-night football game—is informed by and generative of data. How you navigate the internet is informed by data, what items your local grocery store carries is informed by data, and how that football team performs (not to mention what time the game airs and what network you watch it on) is based on data. Anything we do generates information that someone with the desire and skill set can analyze. These analyses are used to make decisions that shape the world around us.

As you can imagine, the amount of data out there exploded with the growth of the internet. Every click, photo, tweet, or post is a data point. According to the nonprofit University of Massachusetts Global, "'Big data' essentially refers to a collection of datasets so large that it cannot be analyzed with normal statistical methods. The Bureau of Labor Statistics explains that such data can include videos, pictures, maps, words, phrases, and numbers. Customer reviews posted on a website, comments and photos logged on a social media platform, electronic medical records and bank records are all examples."[xliv]

What the University of Massachusetts Global calls "normal statistical methods" refers back to Ronald Fisher and the cup of tea. It involves designing an experiment, defining the sample, collecting data, controlling for variables and checking for reliability, and analyzing that data. Big data goes way beyond that. It involves working with data that is not the result of a well-designed, limited study, but rather the result of our everyday actions. As analysis of big data has gotten more sophisticated, so have our abilities to see patterns and make inferences based on the data that has been collected.

Data analysis is a key part of nearly every industry today. Have you ever traveled abroad and gotten a fraud alert from your bank for suspicious activity? Your bank thinks your transactions are suspicious because of big data. Your bank has thousands of data points showing a geographical pattern for your usual transactions, so it recognizes when you break the pattern. Even more than that, your bank has analyzed billions of transactions and knows how likely it is that a foreign transaction in *your* account is fraud. Someone who travels for work wouldn't be getting those notifications, because their bank recognizes that foreign transactions are typical for them.

On a much smaller scale, you are a data analyst in your everyday life. If you are a parent, you know how your child normally behaves. Think of every single interaction you have, every observation you have ever made about your child, as a data point. You know what to expect from them because you have (possibly unconsciously) noticed a pattern in their behavior and made inferences. When your child starts acting differently one day, you suspect they may be sick or have something bothering them, because this new data—their current behavior—doesn't fit the pattern. Maybe the new data leads you to check for a fever or take them to the doctor that day. Your unconscious data analysis has prompted you to change your behavior, to address something differently. This is exactly how big data analysis works in industries, but with a more deliberate approach.

Here's another way big data is used today: chatbots on company websites. Remember last week when you decided to return that pair of pants you had ordered online? You visited the company's website to start a return, and a little box popped up asking if it could help you. You may have thought, sure, but it's 2:00 a.m. on a Tuesday; I'm not sure anybody is working who can help me right now. That little box was generated by artificial intelligence and data—which you probably quickly figured out if you interacted with it. The company knows, from thousands or even millions of customer interactions, what kinds of questions you might have for them. They can then use AI for a chatbot that answers all those typical questions. This saves the company time and money since they don't need to pay someone to answer their customers' most basic and common questions.

The reason those chatbots can exist—that the company has so much data that it can predict and easily answer customers' questions—is the same reason the chatbots can be so incredibly frustrating. Maybe the company predicts, for example, that you are going to ask how to start a return. You might ask if returns are free, how long you have to return an item, or how to generate a shipping label. These are all questions that the company has data on; customers have asked them so many times that the chatbot expects them and can be programmed to answer them. But let's say you have a more specific question, like can you apply the forty-percent-off coupon that you used in your initial purchase to the newly listed green jacket while getting your money back for the pants you want to return. Because it's AI and because this isn't as common a question, the chatbot probably can't answer this. It either tries to answer a different question, leaving you frustrated and maybe slamming your computer closed, or it directs you to call customer service during business hours.

While the results of big data may annoy consumers, most industries think of it as helpful. Data helps them know their customers better so they can target their advertising or products more accurately. In other words, it helps them increase their profit. For sports organizations, big data functions in a similar capacity: it helps them increase efficiency, which leads (hopefully) to better playing and more wins.

Big Data and the Consumer

But what about you, the consumer? Does big data help you?

The answer to this question depends on your viewpoint. You may find it helpful that ads are targeted to your interests when you log into a social media site. Maybe you have found brands you wouldn't otherwise have known about that helped you in some way. Maybe it was easier to find the stylish pair of glasses you wanted because that ad popped up just as you were beginning to think about shopping for glasses. But some people think this incessant data collection is invasive and would rather not have companies keeping tabs on them.

There are small steps we can take to mitigate our data being collected. Most websites now ask you to "accept cookies" when you visit them. These cookies are small pieces of data about you that are stored in your computer's browser—what items you clicked on, for example, or what you put in your shopping cart. You can usually choose to "reject cookies" on a website so that your personal preferences won't be stored. Similarly, you can block location sharing on your phone, since many apps gather information about where you are when you use them. And you can check your privacy settings on social media sites like Facebook, which allows you to customize what information is stored and what can be seen by others.

Even with these precautions, though, you generate data with every move, and there is little you can do to escape being a source besides living completely off the grid. Remember the big Facebook and Cambridge Analytica scandal of the late 2010s? Facebook shared data without its users' permission with a big data company called Cambridge Analytica. Cambridge Analytica used the data mainly for targeted political advertisements, particularly toward those on the conservative end of the political spectrum. Eventually, Cambridge Analytica was found to have provided data on voters to the Trump campaign and was suspected to have given information to Russian political operatives who were trying to influence foreign elections. Mark Zuckerberg, founder and CEO of Facebook, had to answer to Congress about this massive data breach that involved some eighty-seven million users.[xlv]

So as much as you try to avoid having your data harvested, you can only do so much if you are living in the modern world. Everything you do, every click of the mouse, every purchase with your debit card, creates data. This data then gets analyzed and turned around to influence your next move. As *The New York Times* quoted one Facebook user, "You are the product on the internet."[xlvi]

Again, knowledge is power. If you're aware that the ads that pop up on social media are specifically targeted to you, you can more easily resist them. Know that you are constantly generating data and become aware of how that data is used to try to influence you. Then use this knowledge to try to recognize and resist the influences.

Chapter 7

Can A Vaccine Cause Autism? Bad Statistics and How Not To Be Fooled

Now that you've learned that data is all around us and is constantly being analyzed, you may be feeling a bit down, thinking that humanity is just a collection of data points. You may be asking yourself where free will comes into play if your internet browser knows so much about you that it can predict where you're going to make your next purchase. Despite swimming in a sea of data, we need to use our brains to make sure we interpret and use that data correctly. It's tempting to think that numbers don't lie, but analysis is crucial. People make mistakes in data analysis every step of the way—usually unintentionally, but sometimes intentionally.

One of the most consequential misrepresentations of data in recent memory is the 1998 study claiming that vaccines cause autism. Andrew Wakefield and colleagues surmised in a *Lancet* article that the measles, mumps, and rubella (MMR) vaccine led to the development of autism in their small study. Despite the almost immediate refutation of the study by the scientific community, parents around the world latched on to the headline. More than two decades later, pediatricians are still fighting concerned parents' misconceptions, having to convince them that these critical vaccines are harmless. The impact and backlash of this small study was so significant that one 2011 headline reads: "The MMR vaccine and autism: Sensation, refutation, retraction, and fraud."[xlvii]

So what was wrong with Wakefield's study? Wakefield and his colleagues made several key omissions along the way, some of which may have been intentional. According to the Children's Hospital of Philadelphia (CHOP), the study had two main flaws. The first is that administration of the MMR vaccine and diagnosis of autism are typically made around the same time (within the first few years of a child's life). Thus the fact that eight of the study's twelve participants were diagnosed with autism soon after they had received their MMR vaccine could have been purely coincidental. After all, ninety percent of children in the United Kingdom received their

MMR vaccines at that time, but ninety percent of children were not being diagnosed with autism. In order to prove that the vaccine *caused* autism, the study would have needed a control group of children who had not received the vaccine.[xlviii]

The second major flaw, according to CHOP, was in reporting the timeline of events. According to Wakefield and colleagues, the vaccine caused gut inflammation, which then caused symptoms of autism. Upon further examination of the data, though, critics found that the eight children diagnosed with autism complained of intestinal symptoms *after* their autism diagnosis had been made.[xlix] In other words, autism and gut inflammation may have been related, but the timeline of symptoms didn't support the thesis that gut inflammation *caused* autism.

That wasn't the end of Wakefield's story, however. Wakefield and colleagues published a second study in 2002 claiming that the measles virus was found in intestinal biopsies of children with autism. This time they did include a control group that showed that this result was much more common in children with autism than in those without. Critics found even more flaws in this study, including the lack of distinction between the natural measles virus (which was still circulating in the UK at that time) and the virus from the vaccine.[l]

Exposing Fraud

Okay, so maybe Wakefield and his colleagues made a few mistakes and published some sloppy research. It happens quite often in the scientific community, believe it or not. It turns out, though, that Wakefield was being funded by a group of lawyers working on behalf of parents bringing lawsuits against vaccine companies. As the headline read, what began with a simple retraction by the *Lancet* turned into Wakefield being accused of ethical violations and eventually all-out fraud. Wakefield was removed from Britain's General Medical Council, the register of licensed physicians in the UK. The first line of *Wikipedia*'s entry on Wakefield reads: "Andrew Jeremy Wakefield (born September 3, 1956) is a British fraudster, discredited academic, anti-vaccine activist, and former physician."[li]

Wakefield's fraud wasn't immediately recognized by the *Lancet* or by others in the medical community. What brought Wakefield's financial conflicts and the extent of his fraud to light was a dogged journalist named Brian Deer who published several articles exposing Wakefield.[lii] This begs the question of how Wakefield's study—poorly designed, incorrectly analyzed, and fraudulently reported—could have been published in the first place.

A 2011 editorial in the *British Medical Journal* examined Deer's writing on Wakefield to try to expose the flaws in the system. It wasn't just one bad apple (Wakefield), the authors argued, but a systems failure that allowed such a flawed piece of research to gain traction. The authors argue that publishing bad data has major consequences: "Science is our best way of knowing. When work presented as science is shown to be corrupt, it not only discredits that work and its authors, but it also discredits science."[liii] Not to mention the medical consequences: Clusters of measles outbreaks persist as skeptical parents refuse to vaccinate their children. Unfortunately, this isn't the only time medical researchers have failed to serve the population they are entrusted with—far from it. The Tuskegee syphilis experiments also reveal how widely flawed the system of medical research and analysis can be.

Validity, Reliability, and the SAT

Does this mean you shouldn't trust anything? That you should disregard any advice a medical professional gives you, question all science you read, and live solely by what you deem to be true or untrue? No—that would be the pendulum swinging too far in the opposite direction.

The middle ground is that each of us needs to have a discerning eye, whether we are home watching the news or researching a vaccine in a lab. Now that you know a few ways that data analyses can go wrong, make sure what you hear meets certain standards. When you hear results of a study, here are some questions you can ask yourself:

- Is the source unbiased? Are there financial or other reasons to think the source might not be neutral?
- How big was the study? Are the results reproducible on a large scale?
- Does the conclusion seem supported by the data?
- Was there a control group, and were standard scientific procedures followed?

The two big terms we need to think about with data are reliability and validity. Reliability means how well the results of a data analysis (a medical study, for example) can be reproduced. If another study was done on the same topic, would we get the same results? If not, this tells us there may be a flaw in the study's design, perhaps in the sample or population defined. Validity means how valid the results are, or if the data actually proves the conclusion. Believe it or not, reliability and validity are not always there in scientific studies. They're not always there in things that we, as a society, have accepted as fact.

Let's look at some data that is widely accepted: SAT scores. SAT scores are usually considered reliable, meaning a student would get the same or similar score if they took the test multiple times because they are so carefully researched. The SAT uses sample questions and passages to gather data before including anything new in the test. But are the results of the SAT *valid*? Do they tell us what they purport to tell us—how college ready a student is?

The validity of SAT scores has been hotly debated in recent years, particularly since the Covid-19 pandemic began. Pre-pandemic, most colleges in the United States required standardized test scores to accompany an application. As of 2024, only four percent of colleges require them for admission.[liv] This doesn't mean that we have reached a consensus about test scores not being a valid indicator of college readiness. It means, rather, that colleges are recognizing the debate and the effects of the pandemic and choosing not to require them.

Why is the validity of SAT scores so hotly debated? For one, higher scores correlate with higher income brackets. Does this mean that wealthier kids will necessarily do better in college? Many argue that it means the test questions are biased toward more privileged students, who have also had more opportunities for private tutors and test prep classes. The organization FairTest argues that the schools not requiring tests "recognize that standardized test scores do not measure academic 'merit.' What they do assess quite accurately is family wealth, but that should not be the criteria for getting into college."[lv]

On the other side of the argument is the College Board, who argues that SAT scores are "strongly predictive of college performance" and student retention.[lvi] The College Board makes the SAT, though, so it clearly has a vested interest in it being used. If you're using the questions listed above to analyze information, that should raise some red flags. The next step would be to look for other sources and see what they say. In this case, the jury is still out. At least one writer at *Forbes* comes down in favor of the validity of SAT scores: "6 Arguments Against The SAT—And Why They Don't Hold Up" reads a 2020 headline.

What we need to do in this case is read many sources (or even look at the data ourselves if possible) and come to our own conclusions. A PBS article titled "Views of Authorities on Intelligence & Testing" compiled viewpoints of many different academic leaders on this issue. They pretty much all concurred that the SAT does not measure intelligence or even scholastic aptitude, as the decades-old name of the test suggests. Most do believe, however, that there is a correlation between higher test scores and performance in college. But there is no consensus on whether that matters.[lvii] That lack of consensus may be why more and more colleges are giving up the standardized test requirement.

The lesson isn't to disregard all studies or to believe everything you hear. As with most things in life, the answer lies somewhere in the middle. Data can tell us a lot, but it can also be misreported and misrepresented, both unintentionally and deliberately. Ask questions, look at the numbers yourself, and don't believe everything you hear until you've fact-checked it or gotten it from a source you know is reputable.

Chapter 8

Interpreting Correlations - Why People with Big Feet Are Taller Than You

We learned from the last chapter that most experts agree that there is a correlation between higher SAT scores and college performance. A correlation simply means the data falls in a pattern—in this case, higher SAT scores *are often associated with* better performance in college. Correlations do not tell us causation, and they cannot predict individual behavior. If that correlation is true, you can still most certainly have someone with a perfect score drop out of college, or somebody with a very low SAT score become valedictorian. The correlation just tells us that a pattern exists.

Correlation Coefficients

Correlations can be tricky, though, precisely because they don't indicate causation. Correlations come from graphing data from two variables on a coordinate plane, then calculating what is known as the Pearson correlation coefficient (usually represented by the letter r), or how closely related the two variables are. The correlation coefficient can tell us that the two variables are strongly correlated, that they are strongly *negatively* correlated, or that there is no correlation at all (and everything in between).

Correlation coefficients, or r-values, are represented as numbers ranging from negative 1 to positive 1. Think of it as a spectrum. An r-value of −1 means there is a very strong (actually perfect) negative correlation, zero means there is no correlation at all, and positive one means there is a perfect positive correlation.

-1	0	1
Perfect negative correlation	No correlation	Perfect positive correlation

A strong correlation is considered anything between 0.7 and 1. Less than 0.7

means there is some correlation, but the closer the r-value gets to zero, the weaker the correlation.

Perfect correlations, either positive or negative, mean that the two variables are directly linked: Either one rises exactly in step with the other, or one declines exactly as the other rises. It's kind of difficult to produce examples of perfect correlation in everyday life because most phenomena have some variation, even if slight. The number of miles you drive and the amount of gas you use would have a near-perfect positive correlation, since the amount of gas used increases steadily as the number of miles driven increases. This might not be a perfect correlation, though, because several factors influence how much gas you are using at any given moment. (Are you coasting on the highway? Idling at a light? Using the air conditioning?)

A strong negative correlation exists between, for example, the average temperature in winter and the amount of energy used to heat a home. As the temperature increases (assuming it's still cold enough for houses to require heating), the energy used to heat homes decreases. Again this isn't a perfect correlation, because other factors might affect how much energy a given home uses.

What about correlations that are only somewhat strong? Let's look at feet for an example. Have you noticed that your tall friends mostly wear a bigger shoe size than you do? Or maybe you are the tall friend, and you feel like you have clown feet when you stand next to your friends. Most of us would probably guess that shoe size and height are correlated, but we can look at the data to prove it. Here's a graph from StatCrunch showing height on the y-axis (vertical) and shoe size on the x-axis (horizontal):[lviii]

Scatterplot 1: Correlation of Shoe Size and Height

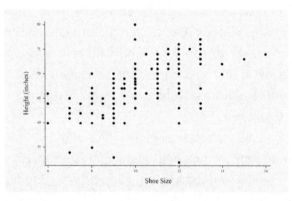

This type of graph is called a scatterplot. Each point on the graph represents one data point, or one person with a shoe size of x and a height of y. You can see that there are points all over the graph, but that they follow an upward pattern as your eye moves to the right. Based on this pattern, we can surmise that there is a positive correlation between height and shoe size. It turns out that, when a linear regression model is run on a calculator or computer, the r-value is .6222.[lix] Remember that the closer the number is to zero, the less strong the correlation, and an r-value of one means there is a perfect correlation. This correlation coefficient tells us that height and shoe size do have a positive correlation, but that it's not perfect—it's not even considered statistically "strong" since it is below 0.7. In real-world terms, this means *most* people who are tall have big feet, but there are plenty of outliers. You could be a shorter person with unusually large feet for your size, or a tall person who happens to wear the smallest shoes among your friends. Either of these would be acceptable, and even expected, with a correlation coefficient of .6222.

A classic example of a strong (but not perfect) negative correlation is car price and age of the car. As cars get older, their cost goes down; a new car will usually cost you substantially more than a ten-year-old one. Just as a positive correlation means that the two variables increase together, a negative correlation means that as one variable (age) increases, the other (cost) decreases. The strength of this correlation varies by car brand, though. Some cars are known to "hold their value" better than others, meaning their value declines less rapidly. Once again, the correlation can tell us what the trend is or what we can expect to be the case, but it allows plenty of room for outliers.

The British website Auto Express gives us two examples of graphs showing car depreciation. The first graph (Car B) is for a typical car that loses much of its value within a year or two of being purchased:

Car B: 10-year depreciation

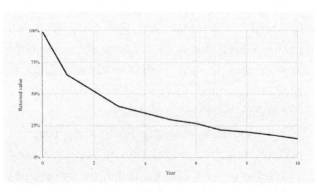

The second graph shows a more linear progression for a car that holds on to its value better, as certain brands are known to do.[lx]

Car A: 10-year depreciation

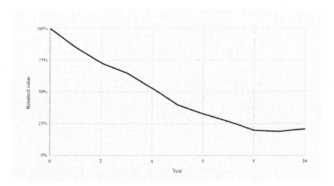

Both of these graphs show a negative correlation between the variables: As the years since purchase increase, the value of the car decreases. Car A shows an almost linear relationship, with the value decreasing pretty steadily over time, while Car B's value drops almost instantly.

Finally, let's look at two variables that have no correlation. Imagine if the two variables we looked at were height and number of pets owned. We would most likely find no correlation there. The graph might look something like this, with each point again representing a single person's data:

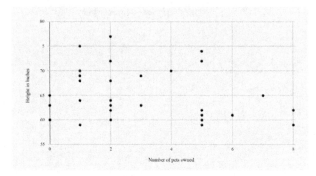

You can tell from looking that there is no correlation between those variables, which makes sense. Height has nothing to do with how many pets a person owns.

Misleading Correlations

Interestingly, we sometimes find a correlation where there is none. Imagine in the example above that my sample—the people I queried—happened to show that greater height was associated with more pets. We would have to think carefully about that correlation and whether it made sense. Was the sample set appropriate? Was the data accurate? Could I repeat the study and get comparable results? Answering these questions would reveal that the correlation was most likely just a fluke. Maybe my sample size was too small, and I happened to get a handful of tall people who have a lot of pets and a bunch of short people with no pets. This inappropriate sampling could suggest a correlation that wouldn't exist if we sampled a larger population.

Incorrect correlations can be fun, but they can also be misleading. Let's look at some fun ones first. There's an entire website, written by Tyler Vigen, devoted to supposed correlations that have nothing to do with each other. He examines, for instance, the correlation between yogurt consumption and Google searches of "i cant even":

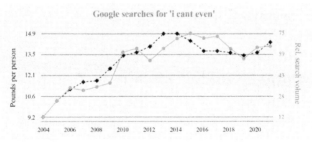

Yogurt Consumption

correlates with

Google searches for 'i cant even'

◆ - - - Per capita consumption of Yogurt in the US . Source: USDA

⊕ —— Relative volume of Google searches for 'i cant even' (Worldwide, without quotes) . Source: Google Trends

2004-2021, r=0.939, r²=0.882, p<0.01 . tylervigen.com/spurious/correlation/2203

As we can see in the graph, those two variables look pretty well correlated—they would likely have a high r-value if he calculated it. He even used artificial intelligence (AI) to come up with an explanation for why this supposed correlation exists: "It's simple. As yogurt consumption rose, so did our tolerance for the sour and curdled aspects of life. It's as if the active cultures in the yogurt fermented a newfound ability to handle all the whey-ward frustrations. So next time you're feeling moody, just grab a spoon and dairy yourself to a better mood. Remember, when life gives you lemons, make fro-yo!"[lxi]

Vigen has even linked each of his graphs to an AI-generated "research" paper. He describes his process on the linked website Spurious Scholar:

Step 1: Gather a bunch of data.

Step 2: Dredge that data to find random correlations between variables.

Step 3: Calculate the correlation coefficient, confidence interval, and p-value to see if the connection is statistically significant.

Step 4: If it is, have a large language model draft a research paper.

Step 5: Remind everyone that **these papers are AI-generated and are not real**. Seriously, just pick one and read the lit review section.

Step 6: . . . publish.

The note after Step 1 claims that he has 25,156 variables in his database. After Step 2, he describes data dredging: "'Dredging data' means taking one variable and correlating it against every other variable just to see what sticks. It's a dangerous way to go about analysis, because any sufficiently large dataset will yield strong correlations completely at random."[lxii]

Data dredging has another term: p-hacking. P-hacking refers to a study's p-value, which is the probability that one could get the same results that the study did by chance. It is used to indicate how statistically significant a study is. The lower the p-value, the greater the statistical significance of a result. P-hacking means dredging a data set until you find *something* that is statistically significant, whether that thing makes any sense or not. Tyler Vigen's "spurious correlations" prove the point that p-hacking is both possible, given enough data, and dangerous, as the results can be incredibly misleading.

Correlation Does Not Equal Causation

It is also possible to have a correlation be true but not causal. In other words, the two variables are indeed linked, but the cause is a third variable that wasn't measured. For example, according to the website Scribbr, ice cream sales and violent crime rates are closely correlated. One might draw incorrect conclusions based on that fact: Maybe eating ice cream leads people to commit crimes, or maybe criminals like to eat ice cream after committing a crime. Both of these seem highly unlikely, though. The correlation exists because a third variable—heat—affects both ice cream sales and violent crimes. When temperatures increase, both of these also increase.[lxiii] So although ice cream sales and violent crimes have a correlation, they don't have a *causal* relationship.

Finally, another problem we encounter when we look at correlated variables is lack of understanding about directionality. For example, researchers have known for many years that depression and vitamin D levels are negatively correlated. In other words, people with low vitamin D levels are often depressed. But researchers are still unclear about causality.

As a 2020 mega-review in the *Indian Journal of Psychological Medicine* put it: "Overall findings were that there is a relationship between vitamin D and depression, though the directionality of this association remains unclear."[lxiv]

Determining causality may seem like a minor point, but it's critical in deciding on a course of action. Doctors may realize depression and vitamin D are linked, but it's unclear if increasing serum vitamin D levels will ease depression symptoms. Should doctors tell their patients to take vitamin D? Or should they focus on other approaches to treating depression and other potential causes of vitamin D deficiency? Causality matters on both an individual and population level. More research is necessary to determine which direction the causality goes and thus what treatments are warranted.

Chapter 9

Program Evaluation and the Retirement of Joe Camel

If you're a Gen-Xer, you probably remember Joe Camel. Joe Camel appeared in Camel cigarette ads from 1988 through 1997. He was supposed to be cool with his cigarette and masculine outfits, often alongside the tagline "smooth character." His job was to entice people to smoke, thereby boosting sales of Camel cigarettes. Joe came under fire in the 1990s, with at least one study showing that the character was as recognizable to six-year-olds as the Disney Channel logo was.[lxv] In 1997, after years of court battles, R.J. Reynolds Tobacco Company voluntarily retired Joe.

The pressure to ban Joe Camel was part of a national panic about teen smoking. Studies showed that teen smoking declined in the 1970s and 1980s but began to rise in the 1990s. Data from high school seniors showed that, in 1990, 19.4 percent of them were "current smokers" (defined as having smoked in the last thirty days). By 1997, that rate had risen to 24.5 percent. Studies have shown that most adult smokers began smoking when they were teens; very few adults pick up smoking as a new habit.[lxvi] All sorts of programs emerged in the 1990s and 2000s to try to reduce or prevent teen smoking, as that was seen as the key to lowering smoking rates overall. If you remember assemblies in school, ad campaigns, or public service announcements about the dangers of smoking, you were the target of one of these programs.

Billions of dollars are spent each year on large-scale programs like the ones to prevent teen smoking. But are these dollars being put to good use? Knowing whether or not these programs are effective is critically important. Nonprofits and governmental agencies do not want to waste billions on initiatives that aren't making a difference. This leads us to another important use for statistical analysis: program evaluation.

Program evaluation, broadly speaking, is the process of figuring out if a program has done what it was created to do. An evaluation of teen smoking prevention programs would tell us whether or not fewer teens smoked, meaning if those billions of dollars spent were worthwhile. A program evaluation might also tell us if certain parts of a program are effective (certain ad campaigns, for example) and if other parts need to be tweaked or discontinued.

A good program evaluation is a thorough, systematic process that uses data to make a determination. According to a guide published by the US Department of Education:

> A well-thought-out evaluation can identify barriers to program effectiveness, as well as catalysts for program successes. Program evaluation begins with outlining the framework for the program, determining questions about program milestones and goals, identifying what data address the questions, and choosing the appropriate analytical method to address the questions. By the end, an evaluation should provide easy-to-understand findings, as well as recommendations or possible actions.[lxvii]

Let's stick with the campaign to reduce teen smoking for now. Program evaluations happened at many points in the process and looked at many different aspects of the campaign. A summative evaluation might tell us how effective the overall campaign was to reduce teen smoking, but other tools were used along the way to tweak the campaign, changing tactics and emphasizing new strategies.

To evaluate the campaign's effectiveness, study designers had to first identify the outcomes they wanted (fewer teens initiating smoking, for example). They had to figure out how they were going to collect the data, and also what kind of data it was going to be. Quantitative data is numbers: Are there actually fewer teens who smoke? Qualitative or categorical data measures things numbers alone can't measure—which ad campaign teens remember seeing, for example. Both are useful, but study designers need to be clear on which type of data will give them the information they want. Program evaluators might also decide to use randomized controlled trials (RCTs) to evaluate a program's effectiveness. You've probably heard of RCTs most with new drugs or medical treatments, as researchers try to determine how effective they are.

According to a meta-analysis published by the National Institute of Health, the teen smoking campaign involved, among other approaches, three major school initiatives: an "information deficit" model in which school-age children were taught about the effects and risks of tobacco, an "affective education" model that emphasized self-esteem and developing values, and a "social influence resistance model" that taught teens how to resist social influences, which included ad campaigns and peer pressure.[lxviii]

Think back to your years in school. Did you have a health or drug-education class that taught you about the effects of tobacco and other drugs? Do you remember attempts to build your self-esteem and influence your health outcomes, like wellness classes or meetings with school counselors? If so, these were likely part of that educational approach. Several studies published in the 1990s and early 2000s showed that, of the three approaches, the social influence resistance model was the most effective. In other words, teaching teens to identify and resist peer and societal pressure had the largest impact (in terms of educational programs) on preventing smoking.[lxix]

Other aspects of the teen smoking campaign included laws targeted at sales of tobacco to teens, penalties for breaking these laws, advertising restrictions, counter-marketing campaigns (ad campaigns about the dangers of smoking, for example), and other community-based interventions. Of these approaches, preventing sales to minors proved to be one of the least effective models. Kids who want tobacco (or alcohol, for that matter) have a way of getting it from older friends and relatives! As of 2004, meta-analyses revealed that the most effective approach was a combined one:

> [The] CDC recommends several components as critical in a comprehensive youth tobacco control program, all of which have parallels in efforts to reduce underage drinking. These components include implementing effective community-based and school-based interventions in a social context that is being hit with a strong media campaign (aimed at some set of "core values") and with an effort to vigorously enforce existing policies regarding the purchase, possession, and use of the substance.[lxx]

Without comprehensive data to back up claims, the smoking prevention campaign might have been abandoned after a few years, or ineffective aspects of the program might have continued while others were terminated. What if someone thought that simply preventing the sale of tobacco to minors would stop all youth from smoking, for example? What if no other intervention programs existed because someone believed so strongly in the power of the law to change behavior? Without an effort to study the data—to systematically analyze the effectiveness of the program—smoking rates today might be as high or higher than they were in the 1990s. As it turns out, in 2023, only two out of every one hundred high school students reported smoking cigarettes in the past thirty days.[3] [lxxi]

Evaluating Healthcare Initiatives

Program evaluation is a critical part of many healthcare initiatives as well. Formative evaluations—meaning ongoing, mid-process ones rather than retrospective ones—have helped shape the Affordable Care Act, first passed in 2010 under President Obama. The ACA attempted a massive reform of healthcare, mandating universal coverage for individuals

---

[3] While cigarette use has greatly declined, other forms of tobacco use are still prevalent, though still at a lesser rate than cigarette smoking in the 1990s.The CDC reports that 10.6% of high schoolers reported using any form of tobacco in 2023. See source [lxxiii].

and attempting to curb costs from providers and insurance companies. Whether or not it succeeded in meeting those goals has been widely debated, with political views often complicating the picture.

Data tells us that the ACA did succeed in getting more people insured: According to the US Census Bureau, 26.4 million Americans remained uninsured in 2022 versus 2013's 45.2 million.[lxxii]

Affordable Care Act Led to Historic Coverage Gains

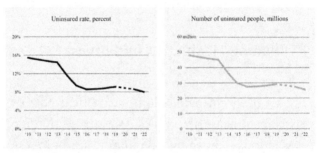

Note: American Community Survey data for 2020 were not released due to disruptions to data collection caused by the COVID-19 pandemic. Dotted line depicts assumption of linear trend between 2019 and 2021.

Source: Census Bureau, American Community Survey

Data also shows that millions more people have access to affordable care, particularly preventive services, and that health disparities between racial and ethnic groups have declined.[lxxiii] Despite these results, legal challenges to the ACA still abound. While the numbers are indisputable, many people oppose the higher premiums individuals have to pay, as well as tax increases that have helped fund expanded care.

This debate over the ACA highlights two potential difficulties of program evaluation. The first is that defining what you are measuring and how to measure it is critically important. Do more people have insurance now than did in 2013? Yes. Are health outcomes in the US measurably better than they were in 2013? That's an entirely different question that would need to be answered with a different set of data. And that's not an easy thing to measure. In evaluating a program, evaluators need to define the outcome they are looking for, figure out how to assess it, and then collect that data. For a massive program like the Affordable Care Act, any kind of evaluation is an enormous undertaking.

The other difficulty program evaluators often stumble upon is a political one. The debate over the ACA hinges on political affiliation, with most liberals supporting it and many conservatives opposing it. With so much data out there and so many potential questions to answer, conflicts over program effectiveness abound. Whatever your argument, you can often find the data to back it up, particularly with such a large-scale program as the ACA. While numbers don't lie, questions can be tweaked or asked in certain ways to get answers that can back up different viewpoints.

So how can you as the consumer of information ensure that you're not being swayed by a particular point of view? Try to make sure the source you get your information from is neutral and doesn't have a vested interest in one particular viewpoint. If you're reading a study that says smoking is actually good for your lungs, for example, ask yourself who paid for that study and who reported it. Was it a major tobacco company that ran the study? Or was it a government health initiative or nonprofit? Always check the source; after all, some advertisements from the 1930s through the 1950s did indeed tout the health benefits of smoking. Ads like the following one were paid for by Philip Morris, the tobacco company[lxxiv]:

Also ask yourself what question the information you're hearing is answering, because the headline might be misleading. One could come up with different evaluations of the ACA based on if one asked about increased coverage, positive health outcomes, or increased taxes, for example. All of these questions are important, but none should be viewed in isolation. Seek out data and analyses from neutral sources and use your own critical thinking skills to make decisions. Just like program evaluators, try not to be swayed by what you want to be true, but look to the actual evidence for information.

Chapter 10

Common Fears and How Statistics Prove Us Wrong

Do you have an irrational fear of shark attacks? Or of air travel? Or of getting stuck in an elevator? We all have fears and neuroses that sometimes govern our behavior. And sometimes we feel so strongly about them that we're truly convinced something terrible is going to happen. I cannot get on that plane, we think to ourselves, because I'm convinced it will go down. Statistics, however, paint a very different picture for many of these fears. If we look at the facts, we may be able to talk ourselves out of some of our most prevalent fears.

Here's a look at five common fears and misconceptions and what statistics can actually tell us about them.

Shark Attacks

Here's an image that might scare you:

SHARK BITES 2023

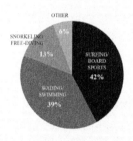

VICTIM ACTIVITY

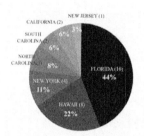

BITES U.S. STATE

You're probably thinking you shouldn't swim in Florida, right? And surfing looks pretty dangerous too.

What this graphic doesn't mention is that those percentages are out of a total of *sixty-nine* shark bites in 2023. And that's worldwide. Only thirty-six of those bites occurred in the United States.[lxxv] So the 44 percent of bites that occurred in Florida means about fifteen people. Now think about the millions of people who visit Florida beaches every year. Fifteen people being bitten in a full year is an exceedingly small fraction of the total.

According to the University of Florida's International Shark Attack File (ISAF), only ten of the sixty-nine bites resulted in death, two of which were in the US.[lxxvi] The Florida Museum of Natural History (Florida has a higher-than-average interest in shark attacks, it seems) calculates this as a one in 11.5 million chance that a beachgoer in the US will be attacked by a shark, and less than a one in 264 million chance that a beachgoer will be killed by a shark.[lxxvii]

If you're still scared, it might help more (unless you're in Australia) to know that the bulk of those ten deaths—forty percent—occurred in Australia, with three of them happening on a remote area of coast known for great surfing. According to ISAF, that coast is home to a large population of seals and white sharks. Sharks like to eat seals, and a surfer flopping about in the water looks an awful lot like a seal to a hungry shark.[lxxviii]

When shark bites do occur, they're big news, and that often stokes fear in people. But they're big news precisely because they're so rare. Think about it: Do you hear about every fender bender on the major highway nearby? No, because they probably happen almost daily. So the next time you hesitate before taking a plunge into the ocean, remind yourself that you're thinking about shark attacks *because* they're so rare. I can't promise that you won't get bitten, but the odds are in your favor that you'll be fine.

Flying

The fear of flying, also known as aerophobia or aviaphobia, is pretty common. It's so common, in fact, that it's listed as a specific phobia in the DSM-5, the definitive guide to psychological disorders. NPR's LifeKit podcast did an episode on it, *Time* magazine has an article on it, and Reddit is filled with threads offering advice to get over it. You may go out of your way to avoid flying, perhaps even driving cross country to see a relative instead of taking a five-hour flight. You may even have the Alanis Morrisette song from 1996 playing on repeat in your head when you board a plane:[lxxix]

Mr. Play-It-Safe was afraid to fly
He packed his suitcase and kissed his kids goodbye

He waited his whole damn life to take
that flight
And as the plane crashed down
He thought, "Well, isn't this nice?"

By now you have probably heard that flying is the safest form of travel. Let's look at the numbers to try to convince you just how much safer it is than driving. According to a Harvard University study, your chances of dying in a plane crash are one in eleven million.[lxxx] That's pretty close to your risk of being bitten by a shark in the waters off the United States. By comparison, your odds of dying in a cataclysmic storm are one in 20,098.[lxxxi] You are more likely to win the lottery than you are to die in a plane crash.

To someone with aerophobia, though, these statistics usually don't mean much. Rationally, they know that flying is incredibly safe, but irrational fears take over. David Ropeik, instructor of risk communication at Harvard's School of Public Health, argues that "risk perception is not just a matter of facts." He points out that all sorts of other factors go into assessing how risky a situation is. For example, maybe a plane crashed recently and you heard about it on the news, so the risk is at the forefront of your mind.[lxxxii] Maybe you had a near crash or other bad flying experience once or heard a story from a friend about a pilot who couldn't do his job safely. Maybe you know that airlines have been struggling financially, so you're worried about pilots being over-extended and airlines cutting safety measures. Any of these concerns—all based on truths—could make flying *seem* much riskier to you than the numbers say it is.

If you're still unconvinced that getting on a plane is safe, many travel magazines offer tips on getting over your fear of flying, and mental health experts are trained to address phobias. But perhaps thinking about the numbers will help calm your fears just a little bit. Once again, numbers don't lie, and comfort can be found in knowing how unlikely your fear is to come true.

Getting Kidnapped by a Stranger

If you have kids, you know the feeling that they are the single most important thing in your life. It's understandable that any kind of threat to your children is terrifying. And there are threats out there, but many of the things we think are major threats are actually very rare.

Let's look at kidnappings, for example. This is many parents' biggest fear, possibly stoked by the years-long campaign that put pictures of missing children on the back of milk cartons. If you are a parent who grew up during these years, you probably spent at least an hour each week staring at the latest picture while you ate your cereal, with little else to occupy your attention.

There are a disturbing number of kidnappings each year in the United States, but the overwhelming majority of them are parental kidnappings. Parental kidnappings, in which one parent absconds with the child without permission (often in fights over custody), are still serious crimes, but they are not the same as a kidnapping by a stranger. Sources put the number of kidnappings per year by strangers between about one hundred and three hundred. If we go with the lower end of that range, that's about twice the number of worldwide shark attacks per year.

A kidnapping, like a shark attack, is another case of an event being in the news because it is so rare. If it happened every day, it wouldn't be news. The news also often reports on "missing children," a phrase that can stop every parent in their tracks. But 95 percent of the time, missing children are children who have run away.[lxxxiii] This is still a traumatic event for their family, but again, it doesn't mean they went missing because a stranger abducted them.

Unless you have a volatile relationship with a family member or co-parent of your child, your child is highly unlikely to be kidnapped. That doesn't mean it never happens, of course, but that the odds are very much in your favor. Again, exercise common sense, but also take comfort in statistics.

Getting Trapped in an Elevator

This one is a bit more complicated. You are most likely not going to get stuck in an elevator, but someone who works in a building with a finicky elevator might tell you otherwise. According to multiple sources, on average, elevators break down once every hundred thousand rides. The chances of an elevator breaking down in a single ride are thus .01 percent. That's really low. If you only ride elevators occasionally, you don't have much to worry about.

However, Elevating Studio, a company that seeks to make elevator riding more efficient, points out that this small risk can add up if you are a frequent elevator user. Let's imagine you live or work in a highrise. If so, you might use the elevator eight times a day. While each trip has a low probability of getting you stuck, you're increasing your odds by riding the elevator so frequently. Elevating Studio calculates that, over forty years of working in a highrise, you have about a six percent chance of getting stuck at some point in your career. If you also live in a building with an elevator, your risk rises to twelve percent over a forty-year period.[lxxxiv] That's not high, but it's not miniscule either.

As with other risks, the risk of getting stuck in an elevator may feel greater to you if you know of someone who was stuck in one. Maybe it was even in your building. And older, less well-maintained elevators are in fact more likely to break down. So if you're a little wary of the rickety elevator in your pre-war high-rise, well, you might have good reason to be.

The good news is that it's highly unlikely for an elevator accident to cause death. You know those scenes in movies where elevators go into free fall, with the hero or heroine barely managing to stop it before it crashes to the bottom of the shaft? Don't worry, that's a Hollywood trope. Elevators have all sorts of built-in mechanisms, including several cables (not just one or two) to prevent them from falling. According to *Wikipedia*, most deaths caused by elevators were in mines or construction sites, where an accident, fire, or other serious malfunction occurred. Though there have been a few deaths and serious injuries in residential or commercial elevators, the incidence remains extremely low.[lxxxv]

Quicksand

Maybe this one only strikes fear in the hearts of people of a certain generation. Classic action movies seemingly wanted people to believe that quicksand was a serious threat to our lives. There is even a 1950 movie called *Quicksand* that portrays the protagonist's descent into a life of crime. According to the trope, quicksand might appear anywhere (especially in a desert), and you'll be powerless against it as it sucks you down below the surface, with bystanders unable to pull you out to safety.

At one point in American film history, quicksand appeared in nearly three percent of movies. It appeared on *Gilligan's Island, The*

Swiss Family Robinson, *The Lone Ranger*, and even *The Lucy Show*.[lxxxvi] Dan Engber, a *Slate* columnist who contributed to a 2013 RadioLab episode on quicksand in Hollywood, went through old movies to figure out just how prevalent quicksand was and came up with the following chart:[lxxxvii]

Percentage of movies with quicksand

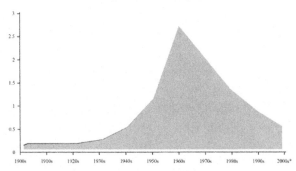

Reality (not necessarily statistics, because there aren't enough of them about quicksand) proves our fears to be irrational. First of all, most people rarely encounter large pools of quicksand, which is really just a fine mixture of sand, clay, and water. Think about when you stand in a tidal pool on the beach and you sink into the sand a few inches, maybe even up to your calves. That's a version of quicksand. Real quicksand can be stickier and

136

deeper than that, but that's the idea. Quicksand cannot, however, suck you under. According to *The Encyclopedia Britannica*, "quicksand is denser than the human body. People and animals can get stuck in it, but they don't get sucked down to the bottom—they float on the surface."[lxxxviii] So even if you do encounter quicksand, you're not going to drown in it the way old heroes and villains did.

Conclusion

You now know a bit about how statistics show up in our daily lives—hopefully more than you did when you started reading this book. You might have been operating for the past ten, twenty, or thirty years thinking that math was just something you learned in school. You might have been one of those students who whined, "But when am I ever going to need to know this?" to their teacher. While you don't need to remember a ton of formulas and procedures to get by in life, it can benefit you to have a basic understanding of how numbers affect us.

Pretty much everything we do can be turned into a data point, and those data points can all be analyzed to make better sense of our lives. Statistical measures help us make better decisions, fine-tune processes, and assess what we have been doing. Knowing a little bit about where statistical analyses come from helps us think more critically and become aware of false claims around us. Just recently, the *Wall Street Journal* reported on the closure of nineteen academic journals due to fake statistics. The publisher of these journals, Wiley, has retracted 11,300 articles over the past two years as they discovered fraudulent data and incorrect conclusions.[lxxxix] Retractions can result from an honest misinterpretation of data or poor review process. In this case, however, these articles were linked to "paper mills," companies that produce "academic" papers with fraudulent data, false authorship, plagiarism, or other violations of academic standards.

So why do paper mills, which exist just for the purpose of publishing false data, exist? The underlying answer is for profit. They can make a profit because people in certain industries, especially academic ones, often gain status or money from publishing. People and institutions that might not otherwise be able to achieve that status can pay to put their name on something that isn't authentic, responsible research.[xc] This practice is becoming ever easier with the creation of artificial intelligence. Publishers are realizing that this is a growing problem, and they need to get savvier about recognizing fraudulent work.

The fact that fraudulent academic work is such a problem speaks to how important data is in our lives. Those who use fake data or slap their name on a plagiarized report do so because they know how influential data can be. You, the consumer of information, are now armed with several tools to help you make sense of data, to recognize when something seems off (there's a correlation between yogurt consumption and Google searches for "I can't even"? Hmm, that doesn't seem right). You know what a difference data can make in our lives, and you can begin to train your eye to find good data.

So now is the time to go forth and put your faith in numbers and science—but only once you have verified that the numbers and science you're looking at come from trusted, unbiased sources, and that they are the results of rigorous statistical analysis. In other words, don't base your decisions on the taste of one or even four cups of tea, but rather on an appropriate sample that gives you reliable and valid data.

Respectfully,

A.R. and Abby Gordon

Before You Go…

I would be so very grateful if you would take a few seconds and rate or review this book on Amazon. Reviews – testimonials of your experience - are critical to an author's livelihood. While reviews are surprisingly hard to come by, they provide the life blood for me being able to stay in business and dedicate myself to the thing I love the most, writing.

If this book helped, touched, or spoke to you in any way, please leave me a review and give me your honest feedback.

Thank you so much for reading this book!

About the Authors

Albert Rutherford

Blind spots can affect our lives without us realizing it. We often try to address our problems, but we rely on incorrect assumptions, faulty analysis, and misguided deductions. This leads to confusion, stress, and annoyance in our personal and professional connections.

Instead of jumping to conclusions prematurely, we can learn to evaluate information correctly and consistently to make better decisions. Developing systems and critical thinking skills can help us collect and assess data, as well as create impactful solutions in any situation.

Albert Rutherford has dedicated his life to finding evidence-based practices for optimal decision-making. His mantra is to ask better questions, to find more accurate answers, and to draw profound insights. In his free time, Rutherford pursues his long-cherished dream of becoming an author. He enjoys spending time with his family, reading the latest science reports, fishing, and pretending to know about wine. He firmly believes in Benjamin Franklin's words, "An investment in knowledge always pays the best interest."

Read more books from Albert Rutherford:
Advanced Thinking Skills
The Systems Thinker Series
Game Theory Series
Critical Thinking Skills

Abby Gordon

After spending the first twenty-five years of her life thinking math was boring and pointless, Abby Gordon began to see the beauty of it. Now she's on a mission to convince everyone that math is 1) relevant; 2) understandable if taught the right way, and 3) an art form that helps us interpret the world around us. She spends her time writing and working as an instructional coach in schools, trying to make math accessible and enjoyable for all.

Abby has an undergraduate degree from Columbia University and graduate degrees from the University of Delaware and Bank Street College of Education. She has spoken at several math education conferences and written on various subjects, including a book on the history of the Horsham Monthly Meeting in Pennsylvania.

When she's not writing or in a school, Abby can be found hiking with her dog or driving the children to their various activities. She is a native Philadelphian who still lives in the area and could happily spend all of her free time in her garden.

List of References

A Guide to Sabermetric Research – Society for American Baseball Research. (n.d.). https://sabr.org/sabermetrics

Askinazi, O. (2023, February 2). *Black people and sickle cell anemia: Your questions answered.* Healthline. https://www.healthline.com/health/sickle-cell-anemia-black-people#how-common

Association Blog. https://nationalcoffee.blog/2023/03/20/celebrate-national-nutrition-month-with-a-cup-of-coffee/#:~:text=Our%20data%20show%20that%2035,alternatives%20and%2027%25%20use%20sugar

Ball, J. (2014, May 25). *How a team of students beat the casinos.* BBC News. https://www.bbc.com/news/magazine-27519748

Bhandari, P. (2023, June 22). *Correlation vs. Causation | Difference, Designs & Examples.* Scribbr. https://www.scribbr.com/methodology/correlation-vs-causation/#:~:text=For%20example%2C%20ic

e%20cream%20sales,to%20creep%20into%20
your%20work

Big data examples: 6 Ways it's transforming
business. (n.d.). *www.umassglobal.edu.*
https://www.umassglobal.edu/news-and-
events/blog/big-data-examples-ways-its-
transforming-business

Blair, G. J. (2023, August 1). Barbenheimer
memes provoke angry backlash in Japan. *The
Hollywood Reporter.*
https://www.hollywoodreporter.com/movies/m
ovie-news/barbenheimer-meme-backlash-
japan-1235548416/

Bonnie, R. J., & O'Connell, M. E. (2004).
*Youth Smoking Prevention Policy: lessons
learned and continuing challenges.* Reducing
Underage Drinking - NCBI Bookshelf.
https://www.ncbi.nlm.nih.gov/books/NBK3760
8/

Brach, E. (2017, October 2). Nick Swisher and
. . . who else? moneyball draftees, 10 years
later. *Bleacher Report.*
https://bleacherreport.com/articles/1284112-
nick-swisher-and-who-the-draftees-of-
moneyball-ten-years-later

Changing Impact. Bat Flips and Nerds.
https://batflipsandnerds.com/2023/09/27/beyon
d-moneyball-the-deep-dive-into-sabermetrics-

and-its-game-changing-impact/#:~:text=The%20Rise%20of%20Saber metrics&text=The%20A's%2C%20led%20by% 20general,like%20the%20New%20York%20Y ankees

Child population by age group | KIDS COUNT Data Center. (n.d.). https://datacenter.aecf.org/data/tables/101-child-population-by-age-group#detailed/1/any/false/1095,2048,574,1729 ,37,871,870,573,869,36/62,63/419,420

Confessore, N. (2018, April 4). Cambridge Analytica and Facebook: the scandal and the fallout so far. *The New York Times*. https://www.nytimes.com/2018/04/04/us/politic s/cambridge-analytica-scandal-fallout.html

Contributor, G. (2023, September 28). *Beyond Moneyball: The Deep Dive into Sabermetrics and Its Game-*

Cousens, M. (2024, March 8). *Most Americans have not seen any of the Oscar nominees for best picture*. Navigator. https://navigatorresearch.org/most-americans-have-not-seen-any-of-the-oscar-nominees-for-best-picture/

Demography - Fertility rates - OECD Data. (n.d.). theOECD. https://data.oecd.org/pop/fertility-rates.htm

Department of Health & Human Services. (n.d.). *Tay-Sachs disease*. Better Health Channel. https://www.betterhealth.vic.gov.au/health/con ditionsandtreatments/tay-sachs-disease

FairTest, & FairTest. (2024, February 21). OVERWHELMING MAJORITY OF U.S. COLLEGES AND UNIVERSITIES REMAIN ACT/SAT OPTIONAL OR TEST-BLIND/SCORE-FREE FOR FALL 2025 - FairTest. *Fairtest - National Center for Fair & Open Testing*. https://fairtest.org/overwhelming-majority-of-u-s-colleges-and-universities-remain-act-sat-optional-or-test-blind-score-free-for-fall-2025/

Famous statistical blunders in history. (n.d.). https://mathcenter.oxford.emory.edu/site/math1 17/historicalBlunders/

Filmfare. (n.d.). *Barbie VS Oppenheimer: Best Fan-made posters of Barbenheimer online.* filmfare.com. https://www.filmfare.com/photos/barbie-vs-oppenheimer-best-fan-made-posters-of-barbenheimer-online-59982.html

French, R. (2023, August 2). *Coffee consumption hits record high in US*. Food & Beverage Insider. https://www.foodbeverageinsider.com/beverag

e-development/coffee-consumption-hits-record-high-in-us

Gardner, M. N., & Brandt, A. M. (2006). "The doctors' choice is America's choice." *American Journal of Public Health*, 96(2), 222–232. https://doi.org/10.2105/ajph.2005.066654

Genetic testing for Jewish First-Time parents - JScreen. (2014, August 21). JScreen. https://www.jscreen.org/learn-more/lifestyle-and-planning/family-planning/first-time-parents/

Groovy history. (n.d.). Groovy History. https://groovyhistory.com/quicksand-facts-movies-tv-history/8

Hammond, C. (2022, February 24). *Can quicksand really suck you to your death?* https://www.bbc.com/future/article/20160323-can-quicksand-really-suck-you-to-your-death

How reliable are elevators and escalators - Elevating studio. (2021, January 14). Elevating Studio. https://elevatingstudio.com/how-reliable-are-elevators-and-escalators/

Howard, H. (2022, February 18). How 1987 Great Storm claimed 18 lives, flattened 15 million trees, and caused £1.5 billion worth of damage—after forecaster Michael Fish infamously told the nation 'don't worry, there

isn't a hurricane on the way.' *Daily Mail*.
https://www.dailymail.co.uk/news/article-
10526903/How-forecaster-Michael-Fish-
infamously-told-nation-not-worry-1987-Great-
Storm.html

Hungary Fires Its Top Weather Officials After
an Inaccurate Forecast. (2022, August 23).
nytimes.com.
https://www.nytimes.com/2022/08/23/world/eu
rope/hungary-weather-forecast-
fireworks.html?smid=url-share

Ibid.

*Interviews - Jon Katzman | Secrets of the Sat |
FRONTLINE | PBS*. (2015, November 18).
https://www.pbs.org/wgbh/pages/frontline/sho
ws/sats/interviews/katzman.html

Irish Demon. (2021, September 07).
Quicksand. Memedroid.
https://www.memedroid.com/memes/detail/346
5591/Quicksand

Jackson, D. (2017, July 7). The Netflix Prize:
How a $1 million contest changed Binge-
Watching Forever. *Thrillist*.
https://www.thrillist.com/entertainment/nation/t
he-netflix-prize

Kean, S. (2023, May 24). *Ronald Fisher, A Bad
Cup of Tea, and The Birth of Modern Statistics*

| *Science History Institute*. Science History Institute Museum and Library. https://www.sciencehistory.org/stories/magazine/ronald-fisher-a-bad-cup-of-tea-and-the-birth-of-modern-statistics/

Kidnapped children make headlines, but abduction is rare in the U.S. (2019, January 11). *Reuters*. https://www.reuters.com/article/idUSKCN1P52BJ/

Liang, J. (2024, February 5). *Shark bites consistent with recent trends, with small spike in fatalities*. Research News. https://www.floridamuseum.ufl.edu/science/shark-bites-consistent-with-recent-trends-with-small-spike-in-fatalities/

McNamara, M. (2024, January 24). Barbie Oscar snubs: Greta Gerwig, Margot Robbie don't get noms - Los Angeles Times. *Los Angeles Times*. https://www.latimes.com/entertainment-arts/awards/story/2024-01-23/barbie-oscar-snubs-greta-gerwig-margot-robbie-movie-point

Menon, V., Kar, S. K., Suthar, N., & Nebhinani, N. (2020). Vitamin D and Depression: A Critical Appraisal of the Evidence and Future Directions. *Indian Journal of Psychological Medicine, 42*(1), 11–21.

https://doi.org/10.4103/IJPSYM.IJPSYM_160_19

Mercer, A. (2024, April 14). *Why 2016 election polls missed their mark | Pew Research Center.* Pew Research Center. https://www.pewresearch.org/short-reads/2016/11/09/why-2016-election-polls-missed-their-mark/

Morrisette, A. (1996). Ironic [Lyrics]. https://genius.com/Alanis-morissette-ironic-lyrics.

Murray, T. (2023, July 24). Oppenheimer received major box office boost because Barbie tickets sold out. *The Independent.* https://www.independent.co.uk/arts-entertainment/films/news/oppenheimer-tickets-barbie-box-office-b2381086.html

Nash, J. (2024, February 14). *Paper Mills—The dark side of the academic publishing industry.* MDPI Blog. https://blog.mdpi.com/2022/05/09/paper-mills/

National SAT® Validity Study— An Overview for Admissions and Enrollment Leaders. (2019). College Board.
nationalcoffee. (2023, March 20). *Celebrate National Nutrition Month with a cup of coffee.* National Coffee

Nietzel, M. T. (2024, February 20). More than 80% of Four-Year colleges won't require standardized tests for Fall 2023 admissions. *Forbes*. https://www.forbes.com/sites/michaeltnietzel/2022/11/15/more-than-80-of-four-year-colleges-wont-require-standardized--tests-for-fall-2023-admissions/?sh=f7d76e97fb96

NOVA | The deadliest plane crash | How risky is flying? | PBS. (n.d.). https://www.pbs.org/wgbh/nova/planecrash/risky.html

Odds of Dying - Injury Facts. (2023, March 1). Injury Facts. https://injuryfacts.nsc.org/all-injuries/preventable-death-overview/odds-of-dying/

Opel, D., Diekema, D., & Marcuse, E. (2011). Assuring research integrity in the wake of Wakefield. BMJ (Clinical research ed.). 342. d2. 10.1136/bmj.d2.

Pannell, R., & Pannell, R. (2023, September 8). *The Danger of averages: Why they can mislead and misrepresent*. LeanScape. https://leanscape.io/the-danger-of-averages-why-they-can-mislead-and-misrepresent/

Penn State. (2021, January 11). Zombie movies and psychological resilience. *ScienceDaily*.

www.sciencedaily.com/releases/2021/01/21011
1190106.html

Philadelphia, C. H. O. (n.d.). *Autism.*
https://www.chop.edu/centers-
programs/vaccine-education-center/vaccines-
and-other-conditions/vaccines-autism

Quicksaaaand! (n.d.).
https://radiolab.org/podcast/quicksand

Rao, T. S., & Andrade, C. (2011). The MMR
vaccine and autism: Sensation, refutation,
retraction, and fraud. *Indian journal of
psychiatry, 53*(2), 95–96.
https://doi.org/10.4103/0019-5545.82529

Reuters. (2023, August 15). China's fertility
rate drops to record low 1.09 in 2022- state
media. *Reuters.*
https://www.reuters.com/world/china/chinas-
fertility-rate-drops-record-low-109-2022-state-
media-2023-08-15/

Roland, J. (2019, August 17). *The pros and
cons of Obamacare.* Healthline.
https://www.healthline.com/health/consumer-
healthcare-guide/pros-and-cons-
obamacare#cons

Royal, J. (2024, February 1). *What income and
wealth put you in the top 1%?* Bankrate.
https://www.bankrate.com/investing/income-

wealth-top-1-
percent/#:~:text=For%20example%2C%20the
%20top%201,than%20%241.52%20billion%20
per%20household

Saperstein, P. (2023, August 11). Nearly a
Quarter of 'Barbie' Filmgoers in the U.S.
Hadn't Been to a Theater Since Before
Pandemic, Survey Finds. *Variety*.
https://variety.com/2023/film/news/barbie-
filmgoers-hadnt-been-theaters-since-pandemic-
1235694530/

Sapkota, A. (2023, August 3). *Dihybrid Cross-
Definition, Steps and Process with Examples*.
Microbe Notes.
https://microbenotes.com/dihybrid-cross/

Science History Institute. (2023, May 24).
*Ronald Fisher, A Bad Cup of Tea, and The
Birth of Modern Statistics | Science History
Institute*. Science History Institute Museum and
Library.
https://www.sciencehistory.org/stories/magazin
e/ronald-fisher-a-bad-cup-of-tea-and-the-birth-
of-modern-statistics/

Spurious correlations. (n.d.).
https://www.tylervigen.com/spurious-
correlations

StatCrunch. (n.d.).
https://www.statcrunch.com/reports/view?repor
tid=35115&tab=preview

Statista. (2024, April 5). *Worldwide box office revenue of "Barbie" 2024, by region.*
https://www.statista.com/statistics/1401601/glo
bal-box-office-revenue-barbie-by-region-
worldwide/#:~:text=As%20of%20Macrh%205
%2C%202024,film%20directed%20by%20a%
20woman

Stewart, J., Joyce, J., Haines, M., Yanoski, D., Gagnon, D., Luke, K., Rhoads, C., & Germeroth, C. (2021). *Program Evaluation Toolkit: Quick Start Guide (REL 2022–112).*
U.S. Department of Education, Institute of Education

Sciences, National Center for Education Evaluation and Regional Assistance, Regional Educational Laboratory Central.
http://ies.ed.gov/ncee/edlabs

Subbaraman, N. (2024, May 14). Flood of fake science forces multiple journal closures. *The Wall Street Journal.*
https://www.wsj.com/science/academic-
studies-research-paper-mills-journals-
publishing-f5a3d4bc

Sullivan, J., Orris, A., & Lukens, G. (2024). Entering their second decade, Affordable Care

Act coverage expansions have helped millions, provide the basis for further progress. *Center on Budget and Policy Priorities.* https://www.cbpp.org/research/health/entering-their-second-decade-affordable-care-act-coverage-expansions-have-helped

Sweezey, A. (2015, April 6). *What does a chance of rain really mean?* WESH 2. https://www.wesh.com/article/what-does-a-chance-of-rain-really-mean/4440726

Team, I. (2023, October 9). *The lottery: Is it ever worth playing?* Investopedia. https://www.investopedia.com/managing-wealth/worth-playing-lottery/

Tech and gaming. (2024, February 7). [Video]. GITNUX. https://gitnux.org/average-number-of-kids-per-family/

The Barbenheimer phenomenon: What social data tells us. (n.d.). Brandwatch. https://www.brandwatch.com/blog/barbenheimer/#

The chemistry of Redheads. (2019, August 21). Let's Talk Science. https://letstalkscience.ca/educational-resources/stem-explained/chemistry-redheads

The Editors of Encyclopaedia Britannica. (n.d.). *How deadly is quicksand?* Encyclopedia

Britannica.
https://www.britannica.com/story/how-deadly-is-quicksand

The math of game shows: Who wants to be a millionaire. (n.d.).
https://artofproblemsolving.com/blog/articles/the-math-of-game-shows

Tsmp, E. F. (2016, August 31). *Moneyball: How big Data & Analytics turned the Oakland A's into the best team in baseball.* TSMP.
https://thesportsmarketingplaybook.wordpress.com/2016/08/31/moneyball-how-big-data-analytics-turned-the-oakland-as-into-the-best-team-in-baseball/

U.S. fertility rate 1950–2024. (n.d.).
MacroTrends.
https://www.macrotrends.net/global-metrics/countries/USA/united-states/fertility-rate

UCL. (2022, October 31). *Ronald Aylmer Fisher (1890–1962).* UCL Division of Biosciences.
https://www.ucl.ac.uk/biosciences/gee/ucl-centre-computational-biology/ronald-aylmer-fisher-1890-1962#:~:text=In%20statistics%2C%20Fisher%20laid%20the,Research%20Workers%E2%80%9D%20appeared%20in%201925

Uk, S. B. W. (2024, January 9). *Boeing blowout: how safe is flying?* Theweek. https://theweek.com/97155/fact-check-is-flying-safe

US Census Bureau. (n.d.). *Explore Census data.* https://data.census.gov/table/ACSST1Y2022.S1901

Vega, N. (2024, March 13). Christopher Nolan earned nearly $100 million from "Oppenheimer" box office and Oscar success: report. *CNBC.* https://www.cnbc.com/2024/03/13/christopher-nolan-earned-a-reported-100-million-from-oppenheimer.html#:~:text=%22Oppenheimer%22%20%E2%80%94%20which%20took%20home,its%2070%2Dmillimeter%20IMAX%20release

Vigen, T. (n.d.) *spurious scholar.* Tyler Vigen. https://tylervigen.com/spurious-scholar

Wikipedia contributors. (2024, April 15). *List of elevator accidents. Wikipedia.* https://en.wikipedia.org/wiki/List_of_elevator_accidents

Wikipedia contributors. (2024, April 2). *Andrew Wakefield. Wikipedia.* https://en.wikipedia.org/wiki/Andrew_Wakefield

Wikipedia contributors. (2024, April 6). *Shark attack. Wikipedia.* https://en.wikipedia.org/wiki/Shark_attack

Wikipedia contributors. (2024, May 10). *Joe Camel. Wikipedia.* https://en.wikipedia.org/wiki/Joe_Camel

Wilkinson, S., & Walker, S. (2024, February 21). Car depreciation explained: future residual values and how they're calculated. *Auto Express.* https://www.autoexpress.co.uk/tips-advice/359491/car-depreciation-explained-future-residual-values-and-how-theyre-calculated

Youth and tobacco use. (2023, November 2). Centers for Disease Control and Prevention. https://www.cdc.gov/tobacco/data_statistics/fact_sheets/youth_data/tobacco_use/index.htm

Endnotes

[i] French, R. (2023, August 2). *Coffee consumption hits record high in US*. Food & Beverage Insider. https://www.foodbeverageinsider.com/beverage-development/coffee-consumption-hits-record-high-in-us

[ii] nationalcoffee. (2023, March 20). *Celebrate National Nutrition Month with a cup of coffee*. National Coffee Association Blog. https://nationalcoffee.blog/2023/03/20/celebrate-national-nutrition-month-with-a-cup-of-coffee/#:~:text=Our%20data%20show%20that%2035,alternatives%20and%2027%25%20use%20sugar

[iii] Kean, S. (2023, May 24). *Ronald Fisher, A Bad Cup of Tea, and The Birth of Modern Statistics | Science History Institute*. Science History Institute Museum and Library. https://www.sciencehistory.org/stories/magazine/ronald-fisher-a-bad-cup-of-tea-and-the-birth-of-modern-statistics/

[iv] UCL. (2022, October 31). *Ronald Aylmer Fisher (1890–1962)*. UCL Division of Biosciences. https://www.ucl.ac.uk/biosciences/gee/ucl-centre-computational-biology/ronald-aylmer-fisher-1890-1962#:~:text=In%20statistics%2C%20Fisher%20laid%20the,Research%20Workers%E2%80%9D%20appeared%20in%201925

[v] Kean, S. (2023, May 24). *Ronald Fisher, A Bad Cup of*

Tea, and The Birth of Modern Statistics | Science History Institute.
https://www.sciencehistory.org/stories/magazine/ronald-fisher-a-bad-cup-of-tea-and-the-birth-of-modern-statistics/

[vi] Science History Institute. (2023, May 24). *Ronald Fisher, A Bad Cup of Tea, and The Birth of Modern Statistics | Science History Institute.* Science History Institute Museum and Library. https://www.sciencehistory.org/stories/magazine/ronald-fisher-a-bad-cup-of-tea-and-the-birth-of-modern-statistics/

[vii] *The Barbenheimer phenomenon: What social data tells us.* (n.d.). Brandwatch. https://www.brandwatch.com/blog/barbenheimer/#

[viii] Blair, G. J. (2023, August 1). Barbenheimer memes provoke angry backlash in Japan. *The Hollywood Reporter.* https://www.hollywoodreporter.com/movies/movie-news/barbenheimer-meme-backlash-japan-1235548416/

[ix] Saperstein, P. (2023, August 11). Nearly a Quarter of 'Barbie' Filmgoers in the U.S. Hadn't Been to a Theater Since Before Pandemic, Survey Finds. *Variety.* https://variety.com/2023/film/news/barbie-filmgoers-hadnt-been-theaters-since-pandemic-1235694530/

[x] Murray, T. (2023, July 24). Oppenheimer received major box office boost because Barbie tickets sold out. *The Independent.* https://www.independent.co.uk/arts-entertainment/films/news/oppenheimer-tickets-barbie-box-office-b2381086.html

[xi] Cousens, M. (2024, March 8). *Most Americans have not seen any of the Oscar nominees for best picture.*

Navigator. https://navigatorresearch.org/most-americans-have-not-seen-any-of-the-oscar-nominees-for-best-picture/

xii *Tech and gaming.* (2024, February 7). [Video]. GITNUX. https://gitnux.org/average-number-of-kids-per-family/

xiii *Demography - Fertility rates - OECD Data.* (n.d.). theOECD. https://data.oecd.org/pop/fertility-rates.htm

xiv *U.S. fertility rate 1950–2024.* (n.d.). MacroTrends. https://www.macrotrends.net/global-metrics/countries/USA/united-states/fertility-rate

xv Reuters. (2023, August 15). China's fertility rate drops to record low 1.09 in 2022- state media. *Reuters.* https://www.reuters.com/world/china/chinas-fertility-rate-drops-record-low-109-2022-state-media-2023-08-15/

xvi Royal, J. (2024, February 1). *What income and wealth put you in the top 1%?* Bankrate. https://www.bankrate.com/investing/income-wealth-top-1-percent/#:~:text=For%20example%2C%20the%20top%201,than%20%241.52%20billion%20per%20household

xvii US Census Bureau. (n.d.). *Explore Census data.* https://data.census.gov/table/ACSST1Y2022.S1901

xviii Pannell, R., & Pannell, R. (2023, September 8). *The Danger of averages: Why they can mislead and misrepresent.* LeanScape. https://leanscape.io/the-danger-of-averages-why-they-can-mislead-and-misrepresent/

xix Statista. (2024, April 5). *Worldwide box office revenue*

of *"Barbie"* 2024, by region.
https://www.statista.com/statistics/1401601/global-box-office-revenue-barbie-by-region-worldwide/#:~:text=As%20of%20Macrh%205%2C%202024,film%20directed%20by%20a%20woman

[xx] Vega, N. (2024, March 13). Christopher Nolan earned nearly $100 million from "Oppenheimer" box office and Oscar success: report. *CNBC*.
https://www.cnbc.com/2024/03/13/christopher-nolan-earned-a-reported-100-million-from-oppenheimer.html#:~:text=%22Oppenheimer%22%20%E2%80%94%20which%20took%20home,its%2070%2D millimeter%20IMAX%20release

[xxi] McNamara, M. (2024, January 24). Barbie Oscar snubs: Greta Gerwig, Margot Robbie don't get noms - Los Angeles Times. *Los Angeles Times*.
https://www.latimes.com/entertainment-arts/awards/story/2024-01-23/barbie-oscar-snubs-greta-gerwig-margot-robbie-movie-point

[xxii] Penn State. (2021, January 11). Zombie movies and psychological resilience. *ScienceDaily*.
www.sciencedaily.com/releases/2021/01/210111190106.html

[xxiii] *Child population by age group | KIDS COUNT Data Center*. (n.d.). https://datacenter.aecf.org/data/tables/101-child-population-by-age-group#detailed/1/any/false/1095,2048,574,1729,37,871,870,573,869,36/62,63/419,420

[xxiv] *Famous statistical blunders in history*. (n.d.).
https://mathcenter.oxford.emory.edu/site/math117/historicalBlunders/

[xxv] Mercer, A. (2024, April 14). *Why 2016 election polls*

missed their mark | *Pew Research Center*. Pew Research Center. https://www.pewresearch.org/short-reads/2016/11/09/why-2016-election-polls-missed-their-mark/

xxvi Jackson, D. (2017, July 7). The Netflix Prize: How a $1 million contest changed Binge-Watching Forever. *Thrillist*. https://www.thrillist.com/entertainment/nation/the-netflix-prize

xxvii Jackson, D. (2017, July 7). The Netflix Prize: How a $1 million contest changed Binge-Watching Forever. *Thrillist*. https://www.thrillist.com/entertainment/nation/the-netflix-prize

xxviii *The math of game shows: Who wants to be a millionaire*. (n.d.). https://artofproblemsolving.com/blog/articles/the-math-of-game-shows

xxix Team, I. (2023, October 9). *The lottery: Is it ever worth playing?* Investopedia. https://www.investopedia.com/managing-wealth/worth-playing-lottery/

xxx Team, I. (2023, October 9). *The lottery: Is it ever worth playing?* Investopedia. https://www.investopedia.com/managing-wealth/worth-playing-lottery/

xxxi Howard, H. (2022, February 18). How 1987 Great Storm claimed 18 lives, flattened 15 million trees, and caused £1.5 billion worth of damage—after forecaster Michael Fish infamously told the nation 'don't worry, there isn't a hurricane on the way.' *Daily Mail*. https://www.dailymail.co.uk/news/article-

10526903/How-forecaster-Michael-Fish-
infamously-told-nation-not-worry-1987-Great-
Storm.html

xxxii Sweezey, A. (2015, April 6). *What does a chance of
rain really mean?* WESH 2.
https://www.wesh.com/article/what-does-a-chance-
of-rain-really-mean/4440726

xxxiii Hungary Fires Its Top Weather Officials After an
Inaccurate Forecast. (2022, August 23). *nytimes.com*.
https://www.nytimes.com/2022/08/23/world/europe/hun
gary-weather-forecast-fireworks.html?smid=url-share

xxxiv Ball, J. (2014, May 25). *How a team of students beat
the casinos.* BBC News.
https://www.bbc.com/news/magazine-27519748

xxxv *The chemistry of Redheads.* (2019, August 21). Let's
Talk Science. https://letstalkscience.ca/educational-
resources/stem-explained/chemistry-redheads

xxxvi Sapkota, A. (2023, August 3). *Dihybrid Cross-
Definition, Steps and Process with Examples.* Microbe
Notes. https://microbenotes.com/dihybrid-cross/

xxxvii Askinazi, O. (2023, February 2). *Black people and
sickle cell anemia: Your questions answered.* Healthline.
https://www.healthline.com/health/sickle-cell-anemia-
black-people#how-common

xxxviii *Genetic testing for Jewish First-Time parents -
JScreen.* (2014, August 21). JScreen.
https://www.jscreen.org/learn-more/lifestyle-and-
planning/family-planning/first-time-parents/

xxxix Department of Health & Human Services. (n.d.).
Tay-Sachs disease. Better Health Channel.

https://www.betterhealth.vic.gov.au/health/conditionsand
treatments/tay-sachs-disease

[xl] *A Guide to Sabermetric Research – Society for
American Baseball Research.* (n.d.).
https://sabr.org/sabermetrics

[xli] Brach, E. (2017, October 2). Nick Swisher and . . .
who else? moneyball draftees, 10 years later. *Bleacher
Report.* https://bleacherreport.com/articles/1284112-
nick-swisher-and-who-the-draftees-of-moneyball-ten-
years-later

[xlii] Tsmp, E. F. (2016, August 31). *Moneyball: How big
Data & Analytics turned the Oakland A's into the best
team in baseball.* TSMP.
https://thesportsmarketingplaybook.wordpress.com/2016
/08/31/moneyball-how-big-data-analytics-turned-the-
oakland-as-into-the-best-team-in-baseball/

[xliii] Contributor, G. (2023, September 28). *Beyond
Moneyball: The Deep Dive into Sabermetrics and Its
Game-Changing Impact.* Bat Flips and Nerds.
https://batflipsandnerds.com/2023/09/27/beyond-
moneyball-the-deep-dive-into-sabermetrics-and-its-
game-changing-
impact/#:~:text=The%20Rise%20of%20Sabermetrics&t
ext=The%20A's%2C%20led%20by%20general,like%20t
he%20New%20York%20Yankees

[xliv] Big data examples: 6 Ways it's transforming business.
(n.d.). *www.umassglobal.edu.*
https://www.umassglobal.edu/news-and-events/blog/big-
data-examples-ways-its-transforming-business

[xlv] Confessore, N. (2018, April 4). Cambridge Analytica
and Facebook: the scandal and the fallout so far. *The
New York Times.*

https://www.nytimes.com/2018/04/04/us/politics/cambri
dge-analytica-scandal-fallout.html

[xlvi] Ibid.

[xlvii] Rao, T. S., & Andrade, C. (2011). The MMR vaccine
and autism: Sensation, refutation, retraction, and fraud.
Indian journal of psychiatry, 53(2), 95–96.
https://doi.org/10.4103/0019-5545.82529

[xlviii] Philadelphia, C. H. O. (n.d.). *Autism.*
https://www.chop.edu/centers-programs/vaccine-
education-center/vaccines-and-other-
conditions/vaccines-autism

[xlix] Ibid.

[l] Ibid.

[li] *Wikipedia* contributors. (2024, April 2). *Andrew
Wakefield. Wikipedia.*
https://en.wikipedia.org/wiki/Andrew_Wakefield

[lii] Rao, T. S., & Andrade, C. (2011). The MMR vaccine
and autism: Sensation, refutation, retraction, and fraud.
Indian Journal of Psychiatry, 53(2), 95–96.
https://doi.org/10.4103/0019-5545.82529

[liii] Opel, D., Diekema, D., & Marcuse, E. (2011).
Assuring research integrity in the wake of Wakefield.
BMJ (Clinical research ed.). 342. d2. 10.1136/bmj.d2.

[liv] FairTest, & FairTest. (2024, February 21).
OVERWHELMING MAJORITY OF U.S. COLLEGES
AND UNIVERSITIES REMAIN ACT/SAT
OPTIONAL OR TEST-BLIND/SCORE-FREE FOR
FALL 2025 - FairTest. *Fairtest - National Center for
Fair & Open Testing.* https://fairtest.org/overwhelming-
majority-of-u-s-colleges-and-universities-remain-act-sat-
optional-or-test-blind-score-free-for-fall-2025/

[lv] Nietzel, M. T. (2024, February 20). More than 80% of Four-Year colleges won't require standardized tests for Fall 2023 admissions. *Forbes*. https://www.forbes.com/sites/michaeltnietzel/2022/11/15/more-than-80-of-four-year-colleges-wont-require-standardized--tests-for-fall-2023-admissions/?sh=f7d76e97fb96

[lvi] *National SAT® Validity Study— An Overview for Admissions and Enrollment Leaders.* (2019). College Board.

[lvii] *Interviews - Jon Katzman | Secrets of the Sat | FRONTLINE | PBS.* (2015, November 18). https://www.pbs.org/wgbh/pages/frontline/shows/sats/interviews/katzman.html

[lviii] *StatCrunch.* (n.d.). https://www.statcrunch.com/reports/view?reportid=35115&tab=preview

[lix] Ibid.

[lx] Wilkinson, S., & Walker, S. (2024, February 21). Car depreciation explained: future residual values and how they're calculated. *Auto Express*. https://www.autoexpress.co.uk/tips-advice/359491/car-depreciation-explained-future-residual-values-and-how-theyre-calculated

[lxi] *Spurious correlations.* (n.d.). https://www.tylervigen.com/spurious-correlations

[lxii] Vigen, T. (n.d.) *spurious scholar.* Tyler Vigen. https://tylervigen.com/spurious-scholar

[lxiii] Bhandari, P. (2023, June 22). *Correlation vs.*

Causation | Difference, Designs & Examples. Scribbr. https://www.scribbr.com/methodology/correlation-vs-causation/#:~:text=For%20example%2C%20ice%20crea m%20sales,to%20creep%20into%20your%20work

[lxiv] Menon, V., Kar, S. K., Suthar, N., & Nebhinani, N. (2020). Vitamin D and Depression: A Critical Appraisal of the Evidence and Future Directions. *Indian Journal of Psychological Medicine, 42*(1), 11–21. https://doi.org/10.4103/IJPSYM.IJPSYM_160_19

[lxv] *Wikipedia* contributors. (2024, May 10). *Joe Camel. Wikipedia.* https://en.wikipedia.org/wiki/Joe_Camel

[lxvi] Bonnie, R. J., & O'Connell, M. E. (2004). *Youth Smoking Prevention Policy: lessons learned and continuing challenges.* Reducing Underage Drinking - NCBI Bookshelf. https://www.ncbi.nlm.nih.gov/books/NBK37608/

[lxvii] Stewart, J., Joyce, J., Haines, M., Yanoski, D., Gagnon, D., Luke, K., Rhoads, C., & Germeroth, C. (2021). *Program Evaluation Toolkit: Quick Start Guide (REL 2022–112).* U.S. Department of Education, Institute of Education Sciences, National Center for Education Evaluation and Regional Assistance, Regional Educational Laboratory Central. http://ies.ed.gov/ncee/edlabs

[lxviii] Bonnie, R. J., & O'Connell, M. E. (2004). *Youth Smoking Prevention Policy: lessons learned and continuing challenges.* Reducing Underage Drinking - NCBI Bookshelf. https://www.ncbi.nlm.nih.gov/books/NBK37608/

[lxix] Ibid.

[lxx] Ibid.

[lxxi] *Youth and tobacco use.* (2023, November 2). Centers for Disease Control and Prevention. https://www.cdc.gov/tobacco/data_statistics/fact_sheets/youth_data/tobacco_use/index.htm

[lxxii] Sullivan, J., Orris, A., & Lukens, G. (2024). Entering their second decade, Affordable Care Act coverage expansions have helped millions, provide the basis for further progress. *Center on Budget and Policy Priorities.* https://www.cbpp.org/research/health/entering-their-second-decade-affordable-care-act-coverage-expansions-have-helped

[lxxiii] Roland, J. (2019, August 17). *The pros and cons of Obamacare.* Healthline. https://www.healthline.com/health/consumer-healthcare-guide/pros-and-cons-obamacare#cons

[lxxiv] Gardner, M. N., & Brandt, A. M. (2006). "The doctors' choice is America's choice." *American Journal of Public Health*, 96(2), 222–232. https://doi.org/10.2105/ajph.2005.066654

[lxxv] Liang, J. (2024, February 5). *Shark bites consistent with recent trends, with small spike in fatalities.* Research News. https://www.floridamuseum.ufl.edu/science/shark-bites-consistent-with-recent-trends-with-small-spike-in-fatalities/

[lxxvi] Ibid.

[lxxvii] *Wikipedia* contributors. (2024, April 6). *Shark attack. Wikipedia.* https://en.wikipedia.org/wiki/Shark_attack

[lxxviii] Liang, J. (2024, February 5). *Shark bites consistent*

with recent trends, with small spike in fatalities.
Research News.
https://www.floridamuseum.ufl.edu/science/shark-
bites-consistent-with-recent-trends-with-small-
spike-in-fatalities/

lxxix Morrisette, A. (1996). Ironic [Lyrics].
https://genius.com/Alanis-morissette-ironic-lyrics.

lxxx Uk, S. B. W. (2024, January 9). *Boeing blowout: how
safe is flying?* Theweek. https://theweek.com/97155/fact-
check-is-flying-safe

lxxxi *Odds of Dying - Injury Facts.* (2023, March 1).
Injury Facts. https://injuryfacts.nsc.org/all-
injuries/preventable-death-overview/odds-of-dying/

lxxxii *NOVA | The deadliest plane crash | How risky is
flying? | PBS.* (n.d.).
https://www.pbs.org/wgbh/nova/planecrash/risky.html

lxxxiii Kidnapped children make headlines, but abduction
is rare in the U.S. (2019, January 11). *Reuters.*
https://www.reuters.com/article/idUSKCN1P52BJ/

lxxxiv *How reliable are elevators and escalators -
Elevating studio.* (2021, January 14). Elevating Studio.
https://elevatingstudio.com/how-reliable-are-elevators-
and-escalators/

lxxxv *Wikipedia* contributors. (2024, April 15). *List of
elevator accidents. Wikipedia.*
https://en.wikipedia.org/wiki/List_of_elevator_accidents

lxxxvi *Groovy history.* (n.d.). Groovy History.
https://groovyhistory.com/quicksand-facts-movies-tv-
history/8

[lxxxvii] *Quicksaaaand!* (n.d.).
https://radiolab.org/podcast/quicksand

[lxxxviii] The Editors of Encyclopaedia Britannica. (n.d.).
How deadly is quicksand? Encyclopedia Britannica.
https://www.britannica.com/story/how-deadly-is-quicksand

[lxxxix] Subbaraman, N. (2024, May 14). Flood of fake
science forces multiple journal closures. *The Wall Street
Journal.* https://www.wsj.com/science/academic-studies-research-paper-mills-journals-publishing-f5a3d4bc

[xc] Nash, J. (2024, February 14). *Paper Mills—The dark
side of the academic publishing industry.* MDPI Blog.
https://blog.mdpi.com/2022/05/09/paper-mills/